Successful Essay Writing

For
English as Second Language (ESL)
Certifications

Templates
Samples
Topic Analysis

Certifications

ECCE/ ECPE
FCE/ CAE/ CPE
IELTS
TOEIC

Stavros Karathanasis
Ph.D., M.Sc.

First Edition 2020

Successful Essay Writing For English as Second Language (ESL) Certifications
Templates – Samples – Topic Analysis

This is the fourth book of this series. Look for the other three books to complete your study.

ISBN: 978-618-84223-4-6 Paper Book

ISBN: 978-618-84223-3-9 (eBook, Kindle Edition)

The front cover photo is created by modifying free distributed photos by Helloquence, and the back cover by Kelly Sikkema, respectively, on Unsplash

Preface

This **series** of **four books** has been designed to help candidates of the various English Language Examinations in use today (**ECCE, ECPE, FCE, CAE, CPE, IELTS, TOEIC**) produce better essays. All these examinations require the candidate to write a text at a proficient level of the English language. However, writing English essays at this level is not something that comes naturally to people. While learning about the process of essay writing is easy, writing good essays is difficult, even for native English speakers, let alone for people whose first language is not English. It requires systematic work and practice.

I do not claim to know everything about essay writing. The knowledge contained in these pages has been acquired during my long-time study of English and is based on a number of very good books and internet sites. I hope this book to assist you accomplish your goal of essay writing learning. The methods discussed in this book are essentially applicable to all essay writing types, regardless of the exam you intend to take.

As it has been already noticed,

Writing is not theory.
It cannot be learned from only reading a book.

It requires practice, making mistakes and learning from them. It takes perseverance. But more than anything else, it takes you actually sitting down writing.

When answering the question asked by the examination process, read it again and again and read it while you are writing your essay so that to be sure you are truly answering it. There is no excuse for losing valuable points or receiving a failing grade simply because you failed to answer the question asked. A grammatically correct writing does not save you if your composition does not answer the topic rubric.

This is the **fourth book** of this series. It is the last book that integrates this Essay Writing Book Series. It uses all essay instructions and essay tips presented in the first three books, and it contains **13** Essay **Templates**, **14 Sample** Essays, **89** Analyzed

Topic, and **48** Topic **Questions**. Along with the other three books of this Series, it is a complete and comprehensive short essays' guide.

In any case, do not hesitate to look for the **other three books**. Only this way will your *Essay Writing Study* be complete.

I wish you good luck with your examination and have a nice time while studying.

Thessaloniki, Greece
January, 2020

Dr. Stavros Karathanasis

When you spot any error, please, let me know be sending me an email, at Karathanasis.Stav@gmail.com, so that to correct it when publishing the next version.

Dedicated
to my children

Katerina, Thalia, Polixeni

Contents

Preface
Introduction

Part I
Templates and Samples

**Part II
Topic Points**

Introduction

An essay is a discussion of a subject of general interest. In it we have to present and justify an opinion about something, offer a solution to a problem, commend on ideas or arguments presented, or speculate about future trends. In Exams for Certifications in **English as Second Language,** Essay questions are written in order to judge the candidate's ability to understand a topic or theme, and to relate general ideas to specific situations.

As the exam is not a time for experimentation you should already know how to plan and write your essay. Of course, there are different ways of making plans, but finding out which way, or ways, work(s) for you before the exam provides you a significant advantage. Therefore, you should write as many essays as possible to make essay writing a habit.

This book has been written to help you (as a student or candidate) to become able to write a good essay regardless of the question asked. This is feasible if you have learned to quick plan your essay and choose the right content.

Part I

Templates and Samples

1. Discursive Essays Structure and Templates

As the exam is not a time for experimentation you should already be able to plan and write your essay in time. Of course, essay questions can be dealt with in many different ways using a variety of words and structures. However, in order to do that in time, you must have developed templates of the most common essay types, and at the time of the exam to seek only for vocabulary related to the specific topic. This strategy may seem simple. However, it is very effective.

Typical essay structures are presented below. They use phrases that can be applied in most essays on different topics. Using phrases like these, the most part of the essay is almost already written before you even start the actual writing process.

When writing balanced essays you must not express strong opinions, instead you have to express clear opinions using impersonal language in order for the essay to sound more academic. To do this effectively you should examine both sides of the argument and consider their merits in turn. Of course, this approach works well when there can be seen merit in both sides of the argument.

Essay's questions that ask for your opinion are formulated in a form like "*To what extent do you believe this is true?*" or "*To what extent do you agree or disagree?*". These questions can be dealt with in a variety of ways. One way is to look at both sides of the argument and then state which one you favor. Broadly speaking there are three different approaches possible in these type of question:

1. I agree (that it is the best answer)
2. I disagree (that it would be effective)
3. I agree and disagree (I accept it but at the same time I say that it would only have a limited effect)

The third answer is often the most intelligent way of answering this kind of questions for many reasons:

1. Answers that say you totally agree or disagree with the proposed point of view ("*completely yes*" or "*completely no*") are typically hard to be organized as you have to explain your arguments in the <u>most</u> part of the essay.
2. Answers that say that the given opinion is partly but not completely true normally provides you with more things to say, giving you, at the same time, the opportunity to write a **for/against** style essay where you can discuss why the proposed point of view might not work and then suggest another alternative.
3. In academic writing, we almost always look at both sides of a question and then come to a balanced conclusion.
4. In balanced essays, you can use more complex grammatical constructions and more sophisticated vocabulary.

It is worth mentioning, again, that any topic can be dealt with in many different ways. In addition, in any topic question, the tasks that can be asked may be different making difficult to cover all possible essay types. For instance, consider the following general information that can be the first part of a topic question about ***genetically modified foods***:

> *"Genetically engineered (or genetically modified) foods such as fruit and vegetables are already being sold in supermarkets. As yet, no definitive studies have been carried out to determine the effect of such foods on humans."*

The possible question's task associated with this topic may be:

1. *"Should this food be on sale when the consequences of consuming it are not yet known? Discuss, giving examples to support your point of view."* (Opinion essay).
2. *"Discuss the advantages and disadvantages of genetically engineered foods."* (For and against essay).
3. *"Discuss the advantages and disadvantages of genetically engineered foods and say whether they should be free to be consumed or should they be banned."* (For and against essay + giving your opinion).
4. *"What are the reasons for such an interest when there is a possible risk of their consumption? And what are the possible consequences on our health"* (cause and effect essay).
5. *"What are the reasons for such an interest when there is a possible risk of their consumption?"* (cause essay).
6. *"What what are the possible consequences of their consumption on our health?"* (effect essay).
7. *"What are the reasons for such an interest when there is a possible risk of their consumption and what are the possible consequences on our health?"* (reasons and consequences essay).
8. *"What can be done by governments and individuals to protect consumers from the possible harmful effects of this kind of food?"* (problem solving essay).

1.1. For and Against Essays

Most common wording of this type of essays is in the form

Statement/Background Information
- *Some people prefer this, while others think that...*
- *Some people do this, while others do something else*
- *Some people do this, while others do not*

Task
- *Do the advantages outweigh the disadvantages of ... (this)?*
- *What are the advantages and disadvantages of ... (this)?*
- *Are there more advantages than disadvantages to do ... (this) rather than ... (this)?*
- *Do you believe the advantages outweigh the disadvantages*

These questions ask you to write whether something is a good or a bad thing. In any case, you must write about both sides of the issue and not only about the disadvantages or advantages because of the way the question may be worded. We can say that the advantages outweigh the disadvantages only if we have considered both. However, in the question *"are there more advantages..."* it does not mean that it is enough to talk about advantages and disadvantages in general, there is a specific question to be answered and you are required to take part, in a more balanced way, though.

The logical approach of these types of questions is to write one paragraph about advantages (pro) and another about disadvantages (con) stating the opinion you agree with first. The basic pattern of this type of essays is "There are two ideas". *"This is the first idea*: it is a good thing" (pros) and *"This is the second idea*: it is a bad thing" (cons). In general, the essay's structure could be:

Introduction
General Statement. Balanced Position
(There are two ideas)
No one can deny the fact that there is plenty of heated debate on the **phenomenon/issue** of...(1), as it has recently aroused much concern among the...(1A) perturbing an important part of the society. However, the issue is far from black and white, so it is worthwhile to investigate it from both sides as it has undoubtedly advantages as well as disadvantages, neither of which should be ignored.

Main body 1
This is the first idea (It is positive)
To begin with, the most serious arguments in favor of...(2) is...(3). Advocates of...(4) draw attention to...(5) as an illustrative example of this phenomenon. In fact, this idea is fully justified by facts both presented on the media as well as published in

international journals. In addition to this, another compelling advantage of...(6), that should not be forgotten, is...(7), pointing out to the fact that...(8).

Main body 2
This is the second idea (It is negative)
On the other hand, a large group of people is convinced that...(9), despite its advantages, also exhibits several limitations, the most significant of which are...(10) and...(11). From their point of view...(12)./From the point of view of those who are opposed to...(12A) on the grounds that...(12B)/ As has already been mentioned, a further common criticism of...(12C) is...(12D). However, the serious drawback in this remark is that it fails to take...(13) into consideration.

Conclusion
Balanced argument
Taking everything into account, it could be concluded that achieving a balance between...(14) and...(15) would be the best course of action, as there are numerous benefits but **crucial/critical** drawbacks are possible as well.

1.2. Essays Discussing two Opposite Views

Most common wording of this type of essays is in the form

Statement/Background Information
- *Many people do ... (this). Others believe ... (that)*
- *Some people believe ... (this), while others regard ... (that)*
- *Some people believe that ... (this) while others think ... (that)*

Task
- *Discuss both views and state your opinion.*
- *Discuss both points of view and give your own opinion.*

In this kind of essays you are asked to compare two opposite views and state which you prefer. It must be noted, that in this case the conclusion is more important than in other type of essays where you just use it to summarize the main points covered in the content paragraphs. You use the conclusion paragraph to add more content by explaining the opinion you outlined in the introduction. So, the essay's structure could be:

Introduction
General Statement. Balanced Position
(There are two ideas)
No one can deny the fact that there is plenty of heated debate on the **phenomenon/issue** of...(1), as it has recently aroused much concern among the...(1A) perturbing an important part of the society. **As a consequence, many people embrace the idea of...(2) while others maintain the standpoint that...(3)./As a consequence,**

some people hold the point of view that...(3A) while others maintain the standpoint that...(3B). However, before we can decide **on/whether**...(4) is...(5), it is worthwhile first to investigate both benefits and drawbacks of the two opinions by considering them from different aspects.

Main body 1 *This is the first idea* (Why people hold the first opinion)
To begin with, advocates of...(6) draw attention to...(7) as an illustrative example of this phenomenon. In fact, this idea is fully justified by facts both presented on the media as well as published in international journals. In addition to this, another compelling reason why a considerable number of people think that...(8), which should not be forgotten, is...(9), pointing out to the fact that...(10).
Main body 2
This is the second idea
(Why other people hold the second opinion)
On the other hand, a large group of people is convinced that...(11), despite its advantages, also exhibits several limitations, the most significant of which are...(12) and...(13). From their point of view...(14)./ From the point of view of those who are opposed to...(14A) on the grounds that...(14B) ...(14C). As it has already been mentioned, a further common criticism of...(14D) is...(14E). However, the serious drawback in this remark is that it fails to take...(15) into consideration.

Conclusion
Balanced argument
Taking everything into account, it could be concluded that achieving a balance between...(16) and...(17) would be the best course of action, as there are numerous benefits in both **points of view** but **crucial** drawbacks are possible as well.

Conclusion taking part
a) However, while it cannot be denied that...(18) both sides should be taken into consideration, as there are valid arguments on both of them.

b) Nevertheless, if I were to choose between...(18A) and...(18B), I would incline to believe that in fact the advantages derived from...(18C) **far outweigh the disadvantages/ may counterbalance the problems it entails.**

1.3. Essays Comparing Two Given Solution to a Problem

Most common wording of this type of essays is in the form

Statement/Background Information
- *... (May be anything)*

Task
- *Do you agree with this policy?*

- *Do you think limits should be set on...?*

If the question refers to ***two solutions*** that are compared in some way, it demands you to talk about both of them using one content paragraph for each one. The essay's structure could be:

Introduction

General Statement
Balanced Position
(There are two ideas. It is "debatable" which of them is the more important or the best)
No-one would disagree that...**(1)** is a serious problem in **the world/many countries**, common to many people's experience and perhaps one of the most critical that **modern societies/teenagers** face today. Subsequently, any proposed solution to this problem presents various difficulties as it is complex. **Accordingly/As a consequence**, many people embrace the idea of...**(2)** while others maintain that...**(3)** is the best course of action. However, in order to be able to decide which solution is more effective, it is highly important to investigate both proposals by considering them from different aspects.

Main body 1

This is the first idea
(Why first point works)
To begin with, advocates of...**(4)** draw attention to...**(5)** as an illustrative example of this phenomenon. In fact, this idea is fully justified by facts both presented on the media as well as published in international journals. In addition to this, another compelling reason why a considerable number of people think that...**(6)**, which should not be forgotten, is...**(7)**, pointing out to the fact that...**(8)**.

Main body 2

This is the second idea
(Why second point works)
On the other hand, a large group of people is convinced that...**(9)**, despite its advantages, also exhibits several limitations, the most significant of which are...**(10)** and...**(11)** From their point of view...**(12)**. From the point of view of those who are opposed to...**(12A)** on the grounds that...**(12B)** ...**(12C)**. As it has already been mentioned, a further common criticism of...**(12D)** is...**(12E)**. However, the serious drawback in this remark is that it fails to take...**(13)** into consideration.

Conclusion

Balanced view
(Both points of view can work perhaps they should be used together)
Taking everything into account, it could be concluded that achieving a balance between...**(14)** and...**(15)** would be the best course of action. On this basis, it can be deduced that the onus is on us to implement the best point of both proposed solutions. This advice, if followed, can make our **society/world** a better and happier place to live in.

1.4. Opinion Essays on Agreeing or Disagreeing with a Given Opinion

Most common wording of this type of essays is in the form

Statement/Background Information
- *It has been argued that...*
- *It is often said that...*

Task
- *Do you agree or disagree with this view?*
- *Do you agree or disagree with this statement?*
- *To what extend do you think this is true?*
- *Do you agree with this policy?*
- *Do you consider this...?*

This is an agree/disagree type question that asks you for your opinion. In fact, there are 2 questions that ask you to do two different things and you have to answer both of them: firstly to discuss both sides of the issue and after that to give your own opinion.

There are, in general, three different approaches possible in this type of question: you could say whether you **completely** agree (it is the best answer/policy), or you **completely** disagree (you do not at all agree that it would be effective/right), or you are somewhere in between (you accept it but you say it would only have a limited effect). The best course of action is the "middle road", to choose something in between discussing the advantages and the disadvantages in the main body and then say in your conclusion that there are both advantages and disadvantages. It is quite always possible, or more exactly it would be better, to answer this type of question by saying that there are equal benefits on both sides of the topic or there are both benefits and dangers associating it. Answering the question by stating that ***you partly agree and you partly disagree with the given opinion***, unless you have strong feelings about the question, allows you

- To use more arguments for both points of view
- To organize your essay in a simple way
- To use some advanced academic language

Actually, this gives you the opportunity to write a <u>for/against</u> style essay. Otherwise, if you decide to totally agree or disagree with the proposal, it is hard enough to organize your main body paragraphs. In the case you feel you have a strong opinion about whether in favor or against the given opinion you should write three body paragraphs providing and justifying three points/reasons why you think so.

In any case, the essay's structure could be:

Introduction

General Statement

Balanced position

(There is one idea which may be right or wrong)

No one can deny the fact that there is plenty of heated debate on the **phenomenon/issue** of...**(1)** as it has recently aroused much concern among the...**(1A)** perturbing an important part of the society. As a consequence, **many people embrace the idea of/ some people hold the point of view that**...**(2)**. However, before we can decide whether it is effective or not, it is worthwhile first to investigate both benefits and drawbacks of this standpoint by considering it from different aspects.

Main body 1

This is the first point of view

(Why people believing in this idea may be right)

To begin with, the most serious arguments in favor of...**(3)** is...**(4)**. Advocates of...**(5)** draw attention to...**(6)** as an illustrative example of this phenomenon. In fact, this idea is fully justified by facts both presented on the media as well as published in international journals. In addition to this, another compelling advantage of...**(7)**, that should not be forgotten, is...**(8)**, pointing out to the fact that...**(9)**.

Main body 2

This is the second point of view

(Why people believing in this idea may be wrong)

On the other hand, a large group of people is convinced that...**(10)**, despite its advantages, also exhibits several limitations, the most significant of which are...**(11)** and...**(12)**. From their point of...**(13)**./ From the point of view of those who are opposed to...**(13A)** on the grounds that...**(13B)** ... **(13C)**. As has already been mentioned, a further common criticism of...**(13D)** is...**(13E)**. However, the serious drawback in this remark is that it fails to take...**(14)** into consideration.

Conclusion

Balanced argument

(Taking part indirectly)

Taking everything into account, it could be concluded that achieving a balance between...**(15)** and...**(16)** would be the best course of action, as there are numerous benefits but **crucial** drawbacks are possible as well. Nevertheless, if I were to choose, I would incline to believe that in fact the **advantages/disadvantages** derived from...**(17) far outweigh the disadvantages/ advantages/may be counterbalanced by the problems it entails.**

Most common wording of this type of essays is in the form

Statement/Background Information
- *One of the major problems facing the world today is... The... should tackle this problem by...*
- *The best way to solve the... problems is to... (do this...)*
- *Recent research shows that... . Some people believe that... is the answer to this problem but others disagree.*

Task
- *To what extent do you agree with this opinion?*
- *To what extent do you agree or disagree?*
- *What is your opinion?*
- *Do you agree with this policy?*
- *Do you think limits should be set on...?*

In this type of question you are given a proposed solution to a problem and you are asked to give your opinion about whether you agree or not that the given course of action would have a positive effect, adopting a clear position on the issue. As in the previous cases, there are, in general, three different approaches possible in this type of question, and your conclusion should reflect the approach you follow. Therefore, in your conclusion paragraph you should say whether you **completely** agree (it is the best answer), or you **completely** disagree (you do not at all agree that it would be effective), or you are somewhere in between (you accept it but you say it would only have a limited effect). The best course of action, unless you have a stronger opinion, is to follow the third choice. In any case, you have to make sure that you will write about the proposed solution looking at both sides of the argument and then give your opinion and not just talk about the problem. You could discuss why the proposed solution might not work and then provide your own alternative solution.

If you choose to follow a more balanced approach to the topic (the third approach), the essay structure may look as follows:

Introduction
General Statement
Balanced position
(The proposed solution may be "a" way of dealing with the problem, but is it the best?)
No-one would disagree that...(1) is a serious problem in **the world/many countries**, common to many people's experience and perhaps one of the most critical that modern societies face today. As a consequence, many people embrace the idea of...(2)

as the best course of action. However, it is arguable whether it is effective or not. Therefore, in order to be able to decide on its effectiveness, it is highly important that we consider it from different aspects, and if it would not be successful to improve the situation of...**(2A)** we should investigate any alternatives.

Main body 1
This is the first idea
(It may be a good idea but it perhaps has possible limitations)
To begin with, advocates of...**(3)** draw attention to the fact that...**(4)** as an illustrative example of this phenomenon. In fact, this idea is fully justified by facts both presented on the media as well as published in international journals. In addition to this, another compelling reason why a considerable number of people think that...**(5)**, which should not be forgotten, is...**(6)** pointing out to the fact that...**(7)**. However, the serious drawback in this remark is that it fails to take...**(8)** into consideration. Therefore, even though it seems to be a possible solution, it is far from an effective method of dealing with...**(9)**.

Main body 2
This is the second idea
(The problems caused from the implementation of the proposed solution necessitate the suggestion of alternative solutions. Discuss why it works better and describe briefly some possible results)
Nevertheless, it is still vital that some **more drastic alternative/supplementary** measures should be taken with the intention of overcoming this problem. Fortunately, there are **many other more/additional** successful ways by which this problem can be dealt with, one of which is the idea of...**(10)**. **Society/Individuals** would be well-advised to do this because...**(11)**. In addition, such an action will result in...**(12)**. Although this might seem a difficult measure to implement, it is our last resort to ensure a solution to the problem of... **(12A)**. Failing to do anything to reduce the impact of...**(13)** on **society/environment** can only lead to worse situations further in the future.

Conclusion
Brief summary of the essay
(The proposed solution may be a good idea but there are difficulties, that is why you suggest an alternative one, mentioning its expected results)
Taking everything into account, it could be concluded that the proposed solution seems to be flawed because they fail to realize the fact that...**(14)**. Subsequently, only by implementing alternative measures can we improve the **society/world** we live in. Nevertheless, even so, the applicability of the alternative proposal presented above would only be possible if...**(15)** and...**(16)** would work together.

Most common wording of this type of essays is in the form

Statement/Background Information
- *One of the most pressing problems facing the world today is...*

Task
- *What... (policies) do you believe... (governments) should adopt to address the causes and effects of this problem?*
- *Should something be done? Discuss and give your opinion.*
- *What measures should both... and... take so as to...?*

This type of essay asks you to find a solutions (or solutions) to a particular problem writing about ways (e.g. policies) to deal with the causes of the problem. In the introduction you need to point out that you are to identify the causes of the problem given and then to suggest solutions needed in order to can deal with problem.

The essay structure may look something like this

Introduction
General Statement
(Point out that you are to identify the causes of the problem and then suggest solutions)
No-one would disagree that...**(1)** is a serious problem in **the world/many countries**, common to many people's experience and perhaps one of the most critical that modern societies face today. Although serious repercussions have arisen as a result of this problem, there are solutions. However, it is critically important to examine some of its main causes before we suggest any possible remedy.

Main body 1
(Investigate possible reasons)
To begin with, it is only the recognition of the reasons for the existence of this problem that makes it easier to solve it. In other word, if **we are to solve this problem/this problem is to be solved**; we must deal with various matters causing it. However, it is not an easy job to identify them. One of the most important factors that contribute to...**(2)** is...**(3)**. Apart from this, we could blame...**(4)** for...**(5)**, but the causes go far deeper than anticipated. In fact,...**(6)** is attributable to...**(7)**. In addition, owing to...**(7A)** (this happened),...**(7B)** (this happens). As a consequence of this,...**(7C)** (this happens). Therefore, it is not unexpected that...**(7D)** is often cited as a typical example.

Main body 2
(Propose solution)
Apparently, if this problem remains unsolved, dire consequences may occur, and, therefore, serious attempts to prevent it must be made. There are several ways by which the problem at hand could be dealt with. In any case, the **first course of action/ first step we need to do** to alleviate this situation is to take measures to...**(8)**. This is advisable because...**(9)**. Another widely adopted way of...**(10)** is to...**(11)**. By taking such measures **we/government/ authorities** can ensure that...**(12)**. This provides a typical instance of...**(13)** and is fully **supported/ justified** by facts.

Conclusion
Balanced view
(Why the proposed solutions can deal with the problem providing evidences why these may be effective)
Taking everything into account, it could be concluded that this problem may seem difficult at first, as there are many causes to be tackled, but it is possible to be dealt with. The above proposal(s), if followed by **individuals, governments and authorities**, can make our **society/world** a better and happier place to live in. After all, it is our responsibility to solve this problem, and we must accept it if the situation is not to get worse.

1.7. Essays Suggesting/ Recommending Course of Action

Most common wording of this type of essays is in the form

Statement/Background Information
- *... (May be anything)*

Task
- *In your opinion who should be responsible for... and what can be done to improve...?*
- *How can... (somebody) render... (this) more appealing to...?*
- *How can... (somebody) sensitize... (somebody else) to do this...?*

This type of essay asks you to suggest who should do something and how should they do this. One possible way to answer this question is to state in the introduction that you are to identify who must do what and mainly how, and in the main body to provide and elaborate three points/solutions/ways of action/recommendations with expected results. Another, alternative, way of dealing with this type of essays resemblances that one used for answering question requiring the suggestion of one or more solutions. In this case, you identify the reasons why (reasons) action must be taken and then describe the course of action.

Another type of similar essays requires you to determine a course of action justifying your decision by giving reasons. Most common wording of this type of essays is in the form

Statement/Background Information
- *... (May be anything)*

Task
- *In your opinion, what should be done for...? What factors affect this...? (why)*

This type of essay asks you to suggest what should be done and why. In the introduction you need to point out that you are going to identify the proposed course of action justifying why you propose this. In the main body, provide and elaborate three main reasons (no causes or effect).

Introduction
General Statement
(Point out that you are to identify the causes of the problem and then suggest course of action and the responsible)
No-one would disagree that...(1) is a serious problem in **the world/many countries**, common to many people's experience and perhaps one of the most critical that modern societies face today. Although serious repercussions have arisen as a result of this problem, there are solutions. However, it is critically important to examine some of its main causes before suggesting any possible remedy and seeking for who is responsible for it.

Main body 1
(Investigate possible causes leading to the problem)
To begin with, a number of factors may account for...(2). However, it is not an easy job to identify them. One of the most important factors that contribute to...(3) is...(4). Apart from this, we could blame...(5) for...(6), but the causes go far deeper than anticipated. In fact,...(7) is attributable to...(8). In addition, owing to...(8A) (this happened),...(8B) (this happens). As a consequence of this,...(8C) (this happens). Therefore, it is not unexpected that...(9) is often cited as a typical example.

Main body 2
(Propose course of action)
Apparently, if this problem remains unsolved, dire consequences may occur, and that is the reason why serious attempts to prevent it must be made. There are several ways by which the problem at hand could be dealt with. Should any action be successful it should be carried out **by any single person/centrally by government/by both individual and authorities**. In any case, the first course of action to alleviate this situation is to take measures to...(10). This is advisable because...(11). Another widely adopted way of...(12) is to...(13). By taking such measures **we/ government/authorities** can ensure that...(14). This provides a typical instance of...(15) and is fully **supported/ justified** by facts.

Conclusion
Balanced view
(Restate thesis and summarize)
Taking everything into account, it could be concluded that this problem may seem difficult at first, as there are many causes to be tackled, but it is possible to be dealt with. The above proposal(s), if followed by **individuals, governments and authorities**, can make our **society/ world** a better and happier place to live in.

1.8. Essays Presenting Causes of a Problem and Evaluating Suggested Solution

Most common wording of this type of essays is in the form

Statement/Background Information
- *... (May be anything)*

Task
- *What are the reasons for this? Should... (somebody)... (do this...) to tackle this problem?*

The first part of the question asks you to identify the reasons why something happens and the second part is a "Yes/No/Maybe" question concerning the applicability of a proposed solution to the problem. As in any case, explain the reason for your answer and deal with the two questions in separate paragraphs.

A similar type of essays arises when the topic ask you to identify the consequences of a phenomenon or problem and to evaluate the effectiveness of a proposed solution to the problem. As in any case, elaborate the possible effects and deal with the two questions in separate paragraphs.

A possible structure might look like this

Introduction
General Statement
(Point out that you are to identify the causes of the problem and then evaluate the suggested solution)
No-one would disagree that...**(1)** is a serious problem in **the world/many countries**, common to many people's experience and perhaps one of the most critical that modern societies face today. This is an escalating issue, and one which has many causes, hence it must be dealt with as effectively as possible. As a consequence, many people embrace the idea of...**(2)** as the best course of action. However, it is arguable whether it is effective or not.

Main body 1
(Explain the reasons leading to the problem)
To begin with, a number of factors may account for...(3). However, it is not an easy job to identify them. One of the most important factors that contribute to...(4) is...(5). Apart from this, we could blame...(6) for...(7), but the causes go far deeper than anticipated. In fact,...(8) is attributable to...(9). In addition, owing to...(9A) (this happened),...(9B) (this happens). As a consequence of this,...(9C) (this happens). Therefore, it is not unexpected that...(10) is often cited as a typical example.

Main body 2
(Say whether the proposed solution would have any positive result or not. Explain why/why not (use conditionals))
Apparently, if this problem remains unsolved, dire consequences may occur, and, therefore, serious attempts to prevent it must be made. There are several ways by which the problem at hand could be dealt with. Advocates of...(11) draw attention to the fact that...(12) is an effective solution to the problem. Though, this idea may seem justified there are some drawback in this remark as it fails to take...(13) into consideration. Consequently, it is far from an effective method of dealing with...(14) and **society/individuals/ governments** would be well-advised to seek for alternatives. To name only one possibly effective measure, they...(15) could...(16) (do this). Although could someone reckon this is a difficult measure to implement, it is a possible resort that can ensure a solution to the problem of...(17).

Conclusion
Balanced view
(Restate why the proposed solutions can deal with the problem providing evidences why these may be effective)
Taking everything into account, it could be concluded that this problem may seem difficult at first, as there are many reasons resulting in it, but it is possible to be dealt with. The above proposal(s), if followed by **individuals, governments and authorities**, can make our **society/world** a better and happier place to live in. After all, it is our responsibility to solve this problem, and we must accept it if the situation is not to get worse.

1.9. Essays Presenting Causes of a Problem and Suggesting Solutions

Another, slightly different, wording of the previously analyzed type of essays could have the form

Statement/Background Information
- ... *(May be anything)*

Task

- *What are the reasons for this? What should... (somebody) do to tackle this problem?*
- *What are the reasons for this and how can... be beneficial?*
- *What are the causes of this phenomenon and what can be done to tackle it?*
- *What are the factors behind this phenomenon and what can be done to alleviate its consequences?*

The first part of the question asks you to give reasons why something happens and the second part asks you to propose one or more possible solutions. Deal with the two questions in separate paragraphs.

A possible structure might look like this (almost similar to that kind of essays presented in paragraph §1.8 with a slight difference in the introduction):

Introduction

General Statement

(Point out that you are to identify the causes of the problem and then suggest solutions)

No-one would disagree that...(1) is a serious problem in **the world/many countries**, common to many people's experience and perhaps one of the most critical that modern societies face today. Although it is an escalating issue, and one which has many causes, there are solutions.

Main body 1

(Investigate possible reasons)

To begin with, a number of factors may account for...(2) However, it is not an easy job to identify them. One of the most important factors that contribute to...(3) is...(4). Apart from this, we could blame...(5) for...(6), but the causes go far deeper than anticipated. In fact,...(7) is attributable to...(8). In addition, owing to...(8A) (this happened),...(8B) (this happens). As a consequence of this,...(8C) (this happens). Therefore, it is not unexpected that...(9) is often cited as a typical example.

Main body 2

(Propose solution)

Apparently, if this problem remains unsolved, dire consequences may occur, and, therefore, serious attempts to prevent it must be made. There are several ways by which the problem at hand could be dealt with. In any case, the first course of action to alleviate this situation is to take measures to...(10). This is advisable because...(11). Another widely adopted way of...(12) is to...(13). By taking such measures **we/government/authorities** can ensure that...(14). This provides a typical instance of...(15) and is fully **supported/justified** by facts.

Conclusion

Balanced view

(Restate thesis and give something to consider)

Taking everything into account, it could be concluded that this problem may seem difficult at first, as there are many causes to be tackled, but it is possible to be dealt with. The above proposal(s), if followed by **individuals, governments and authorities**, can make our **society/world** a better and happier place to live in. After all, it is our responsibility to solve this problem, and we must accept it if the situation is not to get worse.

1.10. Essays Presenting Effects of a Problem and Suggesting Solutions

Most common wording of this type of essays is in the form

Statement/Background Information

- *... (May be anything)*

Task

- *To what extent do you think... (presentation of effects/consequences)? What measures can be taken to...?*
- *What are the effects of... on...? What measures can... (somebody) take to reduce this phenomenon?*
- *Describe some of the difficulties of... and suggest ways to overcome it.*
- *What are the biggest difficulties... (somebody) face(s) when...? How can they be overcome?*

This is also a double questions essay. You must answer both parts of the question using a main body paragraph for each part of it. As it makes sense to talk firstly about the influence of the issue before discussing protection measures, the essay's structure may be:

Introduction

General Statement

(Point out that you are to identify the causes of the problem and then suggest solutions)

No-one would disagree that...(1) is a serious problem in **the world/many countries**, common to many people's experience and perhaps one of the most critical that modern societies face today. Although it is an escalating issue, and one which has many causes, there are solutions.

Main body 1
(Investigate possible reasons)
To begin with,...**(2)** may result in a considerable number of **effects/difficulties**. One of the most important is...**(3)**, that may exert a profound influence on...**(4)**. This, in turn, is bound to result in...**(5)**. In addition,...**(6)** may give rise to a number of extra problems...**(7)** is often cited as a typical but striking example of this situation, which may lead to a far-reaching effect on...**(8)**

Main body 2
(Propose solution)
Apparently, if this problem remains unsolved, dire consequences may occur, and, therefore, serious attempts to prevent it must be made. There are several ways by which the problem at hand could be dealt with. In any case, the first **course of action/ step we need to do** to alleviate this situation is to take measures to...**(9)**.This is advisable because...**(10)**. Another widely adopted way of...**(11)** is to...**(12)**. By taking such measures **we/ government/authorities** can ensure that...**(13)**. This provides a typical instance of...**(14)** and is fully **supported/** by facts.

Conclusion
Balanced view
(Restate thesis and give something to consider)
Taking everything into account, it could be concluded that this problem may seem difficult at first, as there are **effects/consequences** to be prevented, but it is possible to be dealt with. The above proposal(s), if followed by **individuals, governments and authorities**, can make our **society/world** a better and happier place to live in. After all, it is our responsibility to solve this problem, and we must accept it if the situation is not to get worse.

1.11. Essays Presenting Causes and Effects of a Problem

Most common wording of this type of essays is in the form

Statement/Background Information
- *(Introduction of a problem or a situation)... Many people believe that this is due to... (reasons) and leads to...(results)*

Task
- *To what extent do you believe this is true?*
- *What are the factors behind this phenomenon and what are its consequences?*

In this type of essays, you need to discuss cause and effect of a problem. The main body of this essay is a combination of the previously presented types. The essay's structure may be:

Introduction

General Statement

(Point out that you are to identify the results of the problem and then suggest solutions)

No-one would disagree that...**(1)** is a serious problem in **the world/many countries**, common to many people's experience and perhaps one of the most critical that modern societies face today. Apparently, it is an escalating issue which has many causes, and effects on...**(2)**, both of which are worth being thoroughly examined.

Main body 1

(Present possible causes)

To begin with, a number of factors may account for...**(3)** However, it is not an easy job to identify them. One of the most important factors that contribute to...**(4)** is...**(5)**. Apart from this, we could blame...**(6)** for...**(7)**, but the causes go far deeper than anticipated. In fact,...**(8)** is attributable to...**(9)**. In addition, owing to...**(9A)** (this happened),...**(9B)** (this happens). As a consequence of this,...**(9C)** (this happens). Therefore, it is not unexpected that...**(10)** is often cited as a typical example.

Main body 2

(Present possible effects)

Subsequently, having examined the reasons causing this **problem/phenomenon**, it is not difficult to imagine its consequences...**(11)** may exert a profound influence on...**(12)** which, in turn, is bound to result in...**(13)**. In addition,...**(14)** may give rise to a number of extra problems. ...**(15)** is often cited as a typical but striking example of this situation, which may lead to a far-reaching effect on...**(16)**

Conclusion

Balanced view

(Restate thesis and give something to consider)

Taking everything into account, it could be concluded that this phenomenon is due many reasons and results in a significant number of repercussions. Both of them must be considered should there be a solution to the problem of...**(17)**

1.12. Essays Presenting (only) Effect of a Problem

Most common wording of this type of essays is in the form

Statement/Background Information
- *... (May be anything)*

Task
- *What are the possible consequences of...?*
- *How does ... (this) affect... (that)?*

In this type of essays, you need to discuss only the effect of a problem. The main body of this essay could consist of two to three paragraphs presenting and elaborating two to three main results/effects/consequences. The essay's structure may be:

Introduction
General Statement
Indicating Intention
(There are effects)
No one can deny the fact that there is plenty of heated debate on the **phenomenon/issue** of...(1), as it has recently aroused much concern among the...(1A) perturbing an important part of the society. Apparently, it is an escalating issue which has many effects on...(2). These results influence significantly the way we live. Therefore, they are worth being thoroughly examined.

Main body 1
This is the first (group of) effect(s)
To begin with,...(3) may result in a considerable number of **effects/difficulties**. One of the most important is...(4) that may exert a profound influence on...(5) This, in turn, is bound to result in...(6), too. More specifically, the immediate result...(7) can bring about is...(8).

Main body 2
This is the second (group of) effect(s)
In addition to the effect presented above,...(9) may give rise to a number of extra problems deteriorating **the current condition/this matter** even more. ...(10) is often cited as a typical but striking example of this phenomenon, which may lead to a far-reaching effect on...(11). Last but far from least and perhaps one of the most obvious results of...(12) is...(13). Combined with the aforementioned effects, ...(14) may have, the expected outcome is at least an alteration of **the world/life** as we know it.

Conclusion
Balanced argument
(Summarize the main points and give something to consider)
Taking everything into account, it could be concluded that this phenomenon results in a significant number of effects that must be taken into consideration, should there be a solution to the problem of...(15). Only by being aware of the repercussions can we bring about effective measures to be implemented improving the **society/world** we live in.

1.13. Essays Presenting (only) Reasons of a Problem

Most common wording of this type of essays is in the form

Statement/Background Information
- *... (May be anything)*

Task
- *What are the possible causes/reasons of...?*
- *Why do some people do/believe this? What is your opinion?*

In this type of essays, you need to discuss only the reasons of a problem. The main body of this essay could consist of two to three paragraphs presenting and elaborating two to three main reasons/causes. The essay's structure may be:

Introduction
General Statement
Indicating Intention
(There are causes/reasons)
No-one would disagree that...**(1)** is a serious problem in **the world/many countries**, common to many people's experience and perhaps one of the most critical that modern societies face today. This is an escalating issue, and one which has many causes. Therefore, it is critically important to examine some of them, at least the most important, should we be able to suggest any possible remedy.

Main body 1
This is the first (group of) reason(s)
To begin with, a number of factors may account for...**(2)**. However, it is not an easy job to identify them. One of the most important factors that contribute to...**(3)** is...**(4)**. Apart from this, we could blame...**(5)** for...**(6)**, but the causes go far deeper than anticipated. In fact,...**(7)** is attributable to...**(8)**

Main body 1
This is the second (group of) reason(s)
In addition to the reason presented above,...**(9)** may stem from a number of extra sources deteriorating **the current condition/this matter** even more. In other words, owing to...**(10)** (this happened),...**(11)** (this happens). As a consequence of this,...**(12)** (this happens). Therefore, it is not unexpected that...**(13)** is often cited as a typical example.

Conclusion
Balanced argument
(Summarize the main points and give something to consider)
Taking everything into account, it could be concluded that this problem may seem difficult at first, as there are many reasons leading to it, that must be taken into consideration, should there be a solution to the problem of...**(14)**. Only by being aware of the leading causes can we bring about effective measures to be implemented improving the **society/world** we live in.

2. Synoptic Presentation of the Essay Content

Whereas the content of the essay types presented in the previous Chapter may seem different, they have many in common. For this reason, it would be useful to have a synoptic presentation of their content.

2.1. Introduction

A.4. No one can deny the fact that there is plenty of heated debate on the **phenomenon/issue** of...

A.b. No-one would disagree that... is a serious problem in **the world/many countries**, common to many people's experience.

A.1. Advantages and disadvantages: However, the issue is far from black and white, so it is worthwhile to investigate it from both sides as it has undoubtedly advantages as well as disadvantages, neither of which should be ignored.

A.2. Only Causes: This is an escalating issue, and one which has many causes. Therefore, it is critically important to examine some of them, at least the most important, should we be able to suggest any possible remedy.

A.3. Only Effects: Apparently, it is an escalating issue which has many effects on... These results influence significantly the way we live. Therefore, it is critically important to examine some of them, at least the most important, should we be able to suggest any possible remedy.

A.4. Causes and Effects: Apparently, it is an escalating issue which has many causes, and effects on..., both of which are worth being thoroughly examined.

A.5. Causes and propose Solution: Although it is an escalating issue, and one which has many causes, there are solutions.

A.6. Effects and propose Solution (*and doer*): Although serious repercussions have arisen as a result of this problem, there are solutions. However, it is critically important to examine some of its main causes before suggesting any possible remedy (*and seeking for who is responsible for it*).

A.7. Evaluate one given Opinion/Solution/ Proposal: As a consequence, many people embrace the **idea of/point of view that...** as the best course of action. However, it is arguable whether it is effective or not. Therefore, it is highly important that we consider it from different aspects by investigate both benefits and drawbacks of this standpoint.

A.8. Evaluate two given Opinions/Solutions/ Proposals: As a consequence, many people embrace the idea of... while others maintain that... is the best course of action. However, in order to be able to decide which proposal is more effective, it is highly important to investigate both benefits and drawbacks of the two opinions by considering them from different aspects.

A.9. Causes and evaluate proposed Solution: This is an escalating issue, and one which has many causes, hence it must be dealt with as effectively as possible. As a consequence, many people embrace the idea of... as the best course of action. However, it is arguable whether it is effective or not.

2.2. Main Body

14. Pros: To begin with, the most serious arguments in favor of... is... Advocates of... draw attention to... as an illustrative example of this phenomenon. In fact, this idea is fully justified by facts both presented on the media as well as published in international journals. In addition to this, another compelling advantage of..., that should not be forgotten, is... pointing out to the fact that...

1b. Cons or evaluate 2nd Opinion: On the other hand, a large group of people is convinced **that.../this phenomenon**, despite its advantages, also exhibits several limitations, the most significant of which are... and... From their point of view... However, the serious drawback in this remark is that it fails to take... into consideration.

2a/4.1.4. Causes 1st par: To begin with, a number of factors may account for...

2a.1.b. 1st par recognizing causes: To begin with, it is only the recognition of the reasons for the existence of this problem that makes it easier to solve it.

2a/4.2. Rest of the par: However, it is not an easy job to identify them. One of the most important factors that contribute to... is... Apart from this, we could blame... for..., but the causes go far deeper than anticipated. In fact,... is attributable to...

2b. Causes 2nd par: In addition to the reasons presented above,... may stem from a number of extra sources deteriorating the current condition/this matter even more. In other words, owing to... (this happened),... (this happens). As a consequence of this,... (this happens). Therefore, it is not unexpected that... is often cited as a typical example.

34. Effects 1st par: To begin with,... may result in a considerable number of **effects/difficulties**. One of the most important is... that may exert a profound influence on... This, in turn, is bound to result in... In addition,... may give rise to a number of extra problems. ...is often cited as a typical but striking example of this situation, which may lead to a far-reaching effect on... More specifically, the immediate result... can bring about is...

3b. Effects 2nd par: In addition to the effects presented above,... may give rise to a number of extra problems deteriorating the current condition/this matter even more. ...is often cited as a typical but striking example of this phenomenon, which may lead to a far-reaching effect on... Last but far from least and perhaps one of the most obvious results of... is... Combined with the aforementioned effects it may have, the expected outcome is at least an alteration of the world/life as we know it.

3c/4. Effects due to presented causes. Subsequently, having examined the reasons causing this **problem/phenomenon**, it is not difficult to imagine its consequences. ... may exert a profound influence on... This, in turn, is bound to result in... In addition,... may give rise to a number of extra problems. ... is often cited as a typical but striking example of this situation, which may lead to a far-reaching effect on...

5/6. Propose Solution, Doer or alternative:
4. Introduction. Apparently, if this problem remains unsolved, dire consequences may occur, and, therefore, serious attempts to prevent it must be made. There are several ways by which the problem at hand could be dealt with.

b. Doer. (*Should any action be successful it should be carried out **by any single person/centrally by government/by both individual and authorities**.*)

c1. Solution. In any case, the first course of action to alleviate this situation is to take measures to prevent... This is advisable because... Another widely adopted way of... is to... By taking such measures **we/ government/ authorities** can ensure that... This provides a typical instance of... and is fully **supported** by facts.

c2. Evaluate given – propose Alternative: Advocates of... draw attention to the fact that... is an effective solution to the problem. Though, this idea may seem justified there are some drawback in this remark as it fails to take... into consideration. Consequently, it is far from an effective method of dealing with... and **society /individuals/ governments** would be well-advised to seek for alternatives. To name only one possibly effective measure, they... could... (do this). Although could someone reckon this is difficult measure to implement, it is a possible resort that can ensure a solution to the problem of...

7.4. Evaluate (or the *1ˢᵗ*) proposed Opinion: To begin with, advocates of... draw attention to... as an illustrative example of this phenomenon. In fact, this idea is fully justified by facts both presented on the media as well as published in international journals. In addition to this, another compelling reason why a considerable number of people think that..., which should not be forgotten, is... pointing out to the fact that...

7.b. Disagreeing with a given opinion: However, the serious drawback in this remark is that it fails to take... into consideration. Therefore, even though it seems to be a possible solution, it is far from an effective method of dealing with...

8. Describe and Evaluate proposed Solution: To begin with, advocates of... draw attention to... as an illustrative example of this phenomenon. In fact, this idea is fully justified by facts both presented on the media as well as published in international journals. In addition to this, another compelling reason why a considerable number of people think that..., which should not be forgotten, is..., pointing out to the fact that...

9. Propose Solutions: Nevertheless, it is still vital that some **more drastic alternative/ supplementary** measures should be taken with the intention of overcoming this problem. Fortunately, there are **many other more/additional** successful ways by which this problem can be dealt with, one of which is the idea of... **Society/Individuals** would be well-advised to do this because... In addition, such an action will result in... Failing to do anything to reduce the impact of... on **society/environment** can only lead to worse situations further in the future.

2.3. Conclusion

1. Pros/Cons – Two Opinions/Solutions: Taking everything into account, it could be concluded that achieving a balance between... and... would be the best course of action, as there are numerous benefits (*in both **points of view***) but **crucial** drawbacks are possible as well.

1.b.1. Nevertheless, if I were to choose, I would incline to believe that in fact the advantages derived from... **far outweigh the disadvantages/ may be counterbalanced by the problems it entails.**

1.b.2. On this basis, it can be deduced that the onus is on us to implement the best point of both proposed solutions. This advice, if followed, can make our **society/world** a better and happier place to live in.

2. Causes/Effects/Solutions: 4. Taking everything into account, it could be concluded that

2.b.1. the proposed solution seems to be flawed. Subsequently, only by implementing alternative measures can we improve the **society/world** we live in.

2.b.2. this problem may seem difficult at first, but it is possible to be dealt with. The above proposal(s), if followed by **individuals, governments and authorities**, can make our **society/world** a better and happier place to live in.

2.b.3. this phenomenon is due many reasons and results in a significant number of repercussions. Both of them must be considered should there be a solution to the problem of...

2.b.4.a1. this phenomenon results in a significant number of effects that must be taken into consideration should there be a solution to the problem of...

2.b.4.a2. this problem may seem difficult at first, as there are many reasons leading to it that must be taken into consideration should there be a solution to the problem of...

2.b.4.b. Only by being aware of the **repercussions/leading causes** can we bring about effective measures to be implemented improving the **society/world** we live in.

3. Essay Examples

The time provided to complete the writing task in examinations is very limited. Often, it only suffices for the actual writing process and no time is left for extended planning or post-writing checking in order to tackle grammar or syntax errors. Therefore, it is highly important for any candidate to be able to respond to the required task quickly and to the point. Consequently, any candidate should concentrate on the individual aspects and data the given topic question requires and be able to fill in the gaps between them with commonly used and preset, but compelling, material. This action facilitates the candidate and enhances the possibility of getting higher marks.

Use the above presented **Essay Templates** to practice writing essays that can be completed in time while in examination's conditions. The following essays are examples that may follow the above presenting method or not. My intention is to provide you with as many as possible different instances to make you able to respond to any topic question you may encounter.

Some of these essays may be a bit long for examination purpose. Essays written for ECCP or IELTS examinations are shorter, and range between 250-300 words, while essays written for ECCE examinations have about 150 words.

Topic Question: Many parents with talented teenagers do their utmost to exploit these talents and put their children on the road to fame. These parents insist that this offers their offspring great opportunities, guaranteed professional careers and financial security as adults. However, opponents maintain that adolescents are put under too much pressure too early in their lives. What is your opinion on this issue?

No one can deny the fact that there is plenty of heated debate on the phenomenon of young people participation in talent shows, mostly forced by their parents. It has recently aroused much concern among the experts, such as children psychologists, perturbing an important part of the society. As a consequence, some people hold the point of view that children are exposed in stressful situation in an immature age while others maintain the standpoint that this way kids would benefit in their life in long term. However, before we can decide whether it is **a beneficial action or not**, it is worthwhile first to investigate both benefits and drawbacks of the two opinions by considering them from different aspects.

To begin with, advocates of not engagement of kids in talent shows and contests draw attention to the fact that their personality is not fully shaped yet, which is an illustrative instance why they are making so many misleading choices. In fact, this idea is fully justified by facts both presented on the media as well as published in international journals. In addition to this, another compelling reason why a considerable number of people think that kids should be protected from being exposed to excess public attention, which should not be forgotten, is the fragility of their character. They point out to the fact that most children cannot deal with probable failure or rejection damaging their own lives.

On the other hand, a large group of people is convinced that talent competitions concerning children, despite their disadvantages, also provide several benefits, the most significant of which are **future vocational opportunities** and better economic situation. From the point of view of those who are advocate this standpoint, these shows can provide the youngsters with important experience, which is not at all harmful. However, the serious drawback in this remark is that it fails to take the fragile personality and immaturity of most children into consideration.

Taking everything into account, it could be concluded that achieving a balance between **the amount of public exposure** and the protective attitude towards children would be the best course of action, as there are numerous benefits in both standpoints, but crucial drawbacks are possible as well.

(Word Number: 369)

Topic Question: Many people consider attending university to be an important stepping-stone for their careers, for higher income chances, and for living a satisfied life. Do you think that higher education is a necessary step for a successful career and life? Give reasons and specific details to support your viewpoint.

Our contemporary industrial society has created a plenty of occupations requiring specific skills and knowledge. For this reason, many people think that it is very important to be properly educated. This means, qualified at least with a university degree. Therefore, it is worth considering the key reason rendering higher education so important in pursuing a successful career and life.

First of all, higher education provides people, especially young unexperienced people, with knowledge and academic, technical and social skills necessary for the accomplishment of the most demanding tasks, and subsequently, for a successful career. Moreover, higher education enables people do new things that can improve human living conditions and standards, as they will be able to understand the major problems of our modern society and solve them properly. In other words, it gives us the opportunity to become productive and integrated members of our society by acquiring all necessary skills.

Apart from the aforementioned benefits, better earning opportunities and more rewarding jobs, which is the goal of many, if not of the most, people, can be obtained only through higher education, as most highly paid jobs require at least a bachelor degree. This is a key eligibility criterion in many jobs. Last, having higher education it is more possible to can feel security and satisfaction feeling in your job.

To recapitulate, taking everything presented above into account, it is more than obvious that higher education can facilitate us lead a successful working life, and as a consequence a fulfilling personal and family life. Therefore is highly important to make it accessible for as many people as possible.

(Word Number: 266)

Topic Question: Many people consider attending university to be an important stepping-stone for their careers, for higher income chances, and for living a satisfied life. Do you think that higher education is a necessary step for a successful career and life? Give reasons and specific details to support your viewpoint.

Our contemporary industrial society has created a plenty of occupations requiring specific skills and knowledge. For this reason, many people think that it is very important to be properly educated. This means, qualified at least with a university degree. Therefore, it is worth considering the key reason rendering higher education so important in pursuing a successful career and life.

When studying for a degree, more often than not, emerges the need to find the ways to learn by your own, to learn independently. Hence, high educational studies provide us the opportunity to become responsible, to learn how to cope with difficult and unexpected issues, developing our confidence, and affecting positively our self-respect and our personality.

To take thing one step further, higher education may instill important skills in us like self-discipline, organization, and the ability to finish a task from start to finish and on time. In other words, it helps turn us into more professional persons with many work-related skills. Higher education not only trains students in the chosen discipline or field. As studying for a degree entails excessive reading, writing, as well as, presentation of the research outcomes, higher education also teach students how to think analytically, how to understand and handle complex subjects, and, apart from how to solve them, how to communicate them in an effective way. Obviously, this results in improved communication skills, which are important not only for professional purposes, but also for a more successful social life.

To recapitulate, taking everything presented above into account, it is more than obvious that higher education can facilitate us lead a successful working life, and as a consequence a fulfilling personal and family life. Therefore is highly important to make it accessible for as many people as possible.

(Word Number: 292)

Topic Question: Nowadays, more and more people are attracted to and take part in extremely dangerous activities and sports, such as bungee jumping, jumping out of airplanes, speeding on motorcycles, or car racing, especially the young people. **Why do they enjoy experiencing the fear accompanying these activities?**

Some sports are extremely dangerous and entail a high level of risk. Nevertheless, there is an extreme large number of people who still enjoy these activities due to the high adrenaline level they produce and the popularity they provide. There are many reasons accounting for their preference for putting their life to the limits, let us examine some of them.

To begin with, many people in their effort to experience new feelings in their life are willing to take risks and try out new controversial activities, such as those involving extreme excitement or scary, especially when they are popular as well. This way they strive for reducing negative feelings, such as stress and sadness, or releasing the high pressure levels they face in their work environment. To formulate it differently, some people want to escape from the banal daily activities by choosing adventurous games and activities, as these activities bring them a more comfortable and happier mood. They believe that when doing something dangerous, they have to concentrate on it, and, hence, they cannot think about anything else, relieving all the unhappiness they had in their hectic daily life.

Apart from the above presented reason, some people, especially young people, do like to be at risk by their nature. They enjoy facing difficult challenges and overcoming obstacles. As a consequence, they seek to take part in dangerous activities, such as the high-speed car, bike racing, mountain climbing or water sports that increase the adrenaline levels in their bodies giving them extreme enjoyment. This way, they challenge themselves physically and mentally and believe they become stronger by handling life-threatening risks. However, most of them are engaged in dangerous sports and activities for recreational purpose only, since they derive pleasure from them. Despite the fact that the accidents involved in these activities could lead to death or serious injury, they enjoy the pleasure to overcome the danger, especially if it is pre-assessed and controlled. The fun and excitement they are exposed to, they claim, cannot be replaced by the participation in common sports or activities. Extreme sports people tend to perceive fear as something positive and see risks as a mean to push themselves beyond their limits.

Taking everything into account, it could be concluded that there are many reasons leading people to expose themselves in life-threatening activities, that must be taken into consideration, should there be a solution to these problem. Only by being aware of the leading causes can we bring about effective measures to be implemented protecting the participants in extreme sports or dangerous activities.

(Word Number: 426) (Too long for examination purpose. Cut it down!)

Topic Question: Nowadays, more and more people are attracted to and take part in extremely dangerous activities and sports, such as bungee jumping, jumping out of airplanes, speeding on motorcycles, or car racing, especially the young people. **Why do they enjoy experiencing the fear accompanying these activities?**

Some sports are extremely dangerous and entail a high level of risk. Nevertheless, there is an extreme large number of people who still enjoy these activities due to the high adrenaline level they produce and the popularity they provide. There are many reasons accounting for their preference for putting their life to the limits, let us examine some of them.

Peers pressure is an important modulator of risk-taking behaviors, and those who associate with peers that engage in risky activities are more prone to do the same. So, they try dangerous activities to show their peers that they are not cowards and they are not afraid of doing thing that entail high risk levels. Acting this way they get attention, gain recognition, show their friends their particular abilities, they are physically strong and able to overcome their inner fear and weakness, and prove their braveness, confidence and strength. They show that they are fearless and can face any challenge that might seem inevitable. It is only for this reason, why they often take photos or videos to record the moments they play dangerous sports and then post them on the social network for showing. They are really happy when having compliments from their friends, especially the opposite sex. Lastly, group factors play also a huge part in influencing the participation in extreme sports. Many young people tend to take greater risks in a group setting because they derive a sense of belonging and esteem from their membership in groups.

Except for the possible lack of confidence and the need to differ, media also plays a role in attracting young people to dangerous sports. For instance, bungee jumping, diving, wrestling, mount climbing and ice scatting have attained popularity due to their promotion by the media, such as sports magazines, TV sport channels, websites, as well as video games. They are a big contributor to the growth of extreme sports as they dedicate a lot of time and space to action sports attracting constantly new viewers, further increasing their awareness of these sports.

Taking everything into account, it could be concluded that there are many reasons leading people to expose themselves in life-threatening activities, that must be taken into consideration, should there be a solution to these problem. Only by being aware of the leading causes can we bring about effective measures to be implemented protecting the participants in extreme sports or dangerous activities.

(Word Number: 402) (Still too long for examination purpose. Cut it down!)

Topic Question: Nowadays, more and more people are attracted to and take part in extremely dangerous activities and sports, such as bungee jumping, jumping out of airplanes, speeding on motorcycles, or car racing, especially the young people. **Why do they enjoy experiencing the fear accompanying these activities?**

Some sports are extremely dangerous and entail a high level of risk. Nevertheless, there is an extreme large number of people who still enjoy these activities due to the high adrenaline level they produce and the popularity they provide. This is an escalating issue, and one which has many causes. Therefore, it is critically important to examine some of them, at least the most important, should we be able to suggest any possible remedy.

To begin with, some people get attracted to dangerous activities for economic reasons, to earn their living through their participation in adventurous games. In other words, they deem these activities as a job and take them as profession. They are willing to take risk for attracting the public attention, become popular, and earn celebrity status. Once they earn this privilege, they become respectful members of society, and companies, especially sport companies, pay them large amount of money to advertise their products. The abundant amount of monetary income and the astonishing fame to be a global celebrity entails are some of the main reasons driving some people to participate in unsafe sporting activities.

Taking everything into account, it could be concluded that there are many reasons leading people to expose themselves in life-threatening activities, that must be taken into consideration, should there be a solution to these problem. Only by being aware of the leading causes can we bring about effective measures to be implemented protecting the participants in extreme sports or dangerous activities.

(Word Number: 247)

Topic Question: Extreme sports, also called action, adventurous, or adventure sports, are associated with a high level of risk or danger. However, despite the risks involved, people's participation in them has increased dramatically nowadays. Give some **suggestions** on **how** can extreme sports participants deal with these dangers.

No-one would disagree that the repercussions of participating in risky sports or activities, such as car racing, or diving, is a serious problem in the world, common to many young people's experience. Although serious repercussions have arisen as a result of this action, there are solutions. However, it is critically important to examine some of its main results before we suggest any possible remedy.

To begin with, participating in dangerous sports and activities may have a considerable number of repercussions. One of the most important is life-threatening injuries that may exert a profound influence on the quality of life of the participants, if not claim their life itself. This, in turn, is bound to result at least in increased hospitalization or medical treatment costs, too, apart from the casualties themselves.

Apparently, if this problem remains unsolved, dire consequences may occur, and, therefore, serious attempts to prevent it must be made. There are several ways by which the issue at hand could be dealt with. In any case, the **first course of action** to alleviate this situation is to make safety measures and rules mandatory. This is advisable because many accidents take place due to inappropriate equipment and extreme self-confidence. Another widely adopted way of preventing fatalities is to impose proper train by law. By taking such measures **we, the government, and the corresponding authorities** can ensure that extreme sport and activities will be less dangerous.

Taking everything into account, it could be concluded that the repercussions of these activities and sports may seem unbearable and inevitable at first, but it is possible to be dealt with. The above proposals, if followed by **individuals, governments and authorities**, can make our **society** a better and happier place to live in, as participating in extreme sports and adventure activities will be safer. After all, it is our responsibility to solve this issue, and we must accept it if the situation is not to get worse.

(Word Number: 322)

Topic Question: Extreme sports, also called action, adventurous, or adventure sports, are associated with a high level of risk or danger. However, despite the risks involved, people's participation in them has increased dramatically nowadays. Give some **suggestions** on **how** can extreme sports participants deal with these dangers.

Despite the fact that there are many risks associated with extreme sports and adventure activities, many people do not only love them but also adore them because of the feeling of achievement and the celebrity status they provide. As the participation in such activities can be characterized as a very enjoyable but dangerous experience, some restrictions should be imposed and steps be taken by governments and authorities to control the involving danger and render these activities safer.

To begin with, the first course of action to alleviate the repercussion of these activities would be to prohibit small children and young people from practicing this kind of sports, because they are not mature enough to deal with the dangers they entail. In addition, uncontrolled games, sports, or activities of any kind that risk people's' lives should be banned by law.

To control the repercussions of practicing extreme sports and the participation in adventure activities, standardization of them by putting strict rules, compulsory training by professional and experienced coaches and preliminary equipment tests are necessary processes to minimize any possible danger that may occur. Extensive training could take place in a simulated environment so that the participants know beforehand what they should or not do, and get an overall idea about dangers associated with these sports. Following strict safety rules, taking proper precautions according to standard guidelines, having good preparation, learning from the experience of others and joining a group rather than attempting them individually, are essential prerequisites to be able to play these sports or enjoy these activities safely.

Taking everything into account, it could be concluded that the repercussions of these activities and sports may seem unbearable and inevitable at first, but it is possible to be dealt with. The above proposals, if followed by **individuals, governments and authorities**, can make our **society** a better and happier place to live in, as participating in extreme sports and adventure activities will be safer and really enjoyable.

(Word Number: 325)

Topic Question: It is said that humans have an innate need to belong to groups because they are highly social beings. What are some of the reasons that motivate them to do so?

Groups, either they are very small of just two people or very large of many people, are the fundamental component of society and maintain the social life we are aware of. However, why do people seek to form groups and live together with other humans? Let try to examine some possible reasons.

To begin with, we humans, as social beings, understand ourselves and our place in the world only with reference to other people, and in relation to the groups we belong in. These groups influence, or still determine, our identity. For this reason, people join groups and associate themselves with the traits of the other members, conveying a certain social identity. In such cases, it is not rare for the individuals to display their connections with these groups to other people so that let them know their particular features. Moreover, some persons might join a group to gain a sense of purpose in their life. Since groups usually have a common purpose, the person who belongs to them enjoys the feeling that this way their life is more meaningful.

Lastly, it is worth mentioning that the complexity of human life is another important cause that forces us form different groups with various purposes and goals. When living in groups, survival chances are increased and the sense of security is enhanced. In addition, almost everything we produce is possible only through collective action. It is more than obvious that groups of people with a common purpose have the capability to achieve more things than individuals can do alone.

Taking everything into account, it could be concluded that forming and participating in groups is a key process if we would like to live a more fulfilling life. By appreciating what is going on in groups we can to make them more beneficial to their members as well as to society as a whole.

(Word Number: 312)

Topic Question: It is said that humans have an innate need to belong to groups because they are highly social beings. What are some of the reasons that motivate them to do so?

Groups, either they are very small of just two people or very large of many people, are the fundamental component of society and maintain the social life we are aware of. However, why do people seek to form groups and live together with other humans? Let try to examine some possible reasons.

To begin with, some people might join a group simply to be in the company with other people. This way, they feel better, since loneliness is one of the most unpleasant emotions humans can experience. It is a common place that being alone makes individuals feel weak, lost, disconnected, and less worthy. For this reason, most of us try to make sure that we are part of one social group, or preferably of more. In fact, we all are a member of the smallest social group, although not voluntary, the family.

Taking everything into account, it could be concluded that forming and participating in groups is a key process if we would like to live a more fulfilling life. By appreciating what is going on in groups we can to make them more beneficial to their members as well as to society as a whole.

(Word Number: 197)

Topic Question: Some people get dressed in clothes that most people would consider unusual. What our clothes might be saying about us? What effect does a person's appearance have on other people? Discuss, and give specific examples to support your views.

It is a common believe that people are first judged by their physical attributes and clothing. However, if it is true, how important is dressing well in making a good impression? Let us take a short look.

First impressions are often more significant than we might can think. What we wear conveys a large amount of information about us in just a few seconds. In other words, our clothes make a huge difference to what people will think about us. Since we make hasty judgments about people from the clothes they wear, some people can be characterized as friendly, efficient, extrovert, simply by the way they are dressed. So, it is worthwhile to use a certain dressing codes to impress our peers, or other people for specific purposes. In fact, it could be the key to success.

Thus, despite the fact that for many people what they wear is merely a matter of habit, we all should be a little more careful in the choices we make. This is important because most people make all sorts of assessments, assumptions and decisions about the others in the first few seconds of seeing them, and actually without proper evidence. Therefore, to take things one step further, by doing something different with our clothes might be a way of changing the impression other people have of us.

Taking everything into account, because our clothes say a great deal about who we are, and can convey a great deal of socially important things to others, even if this impression is actually unfounded, it is important to choose our style carefully.

(Word Number: 266)

Topic Question: Some people modify their body using tattoos and body piercings. Most people consider this strange. Why do people decorate themselves in ways that make them stand out from the crowd? Discuss, and give specific examples to support your views.

Instead of a new hair cut or color, or maybe even a new pair of shoes or a new shirt, today's younger generation is particularly interested in another, new, form of expression: tattoos and body piercing. As there may be a lot of reasons accounting for this phenomenon, let us examine a few of them.

To begin with, some people consider tattoos and body piercing as a fashionable form of body art, which helps them make a personal statement. It is a way of expressing their selves in a way that renders their self-image more individual. On the other hand, there are some other people that use tattoos to remember somebody or something important in their life. In these cases, tattoos have a personal meaning. However, in any case, the point of a tattoo is to show others the meaning of choosing to do so.

Another cause that may lead people get a tattoo is to show rebellion. Mostly young adults choose to get a tattoo to display their disapproval of the society, or even their parents. These people express themselves through decorating their skin with tattoos, piercings and other forms of body art using certain symbolisms. For this reason, tattoos have been associated to certain groups of people, reflecting their behavior.

Taking everything into account, we can conclude that whether it is to remember something great that happened in people's life, to show affection or emotion, or because that specific design meant a lot to them, there are many reasons for a tattoo.

(Word Number: 254)

Topic Question: Human beings have kept animals since the earliest times. What are the benefits and disadvantages of pet ownership?

Keeping companion animals plays an important role to the life of their owner as these animals can form close bond with their owner. However, pet ownership is a far from black and white issue, so that it is worthwhile to investigate it from both sides as it has undoubtedly advantages as well as disadvantages, neither of which should be ignored.

To begin with, the most serious arguments in favor of having a pet is pets reduce stress and people will be more relaxed after spending time with their pets. Advocates of pet ownership draw attention to the fact that dogs and cats are very close to humans for thousands of years, as an illustrative example of their opinion. In addition to this, another compelling advantage of companion animals, that should not be forgotten, is that they can help people keep healthy. They point out to the fact that since, for instance, dogs need lots of exercise to keep fit and healthy, most dog owners have to allocate time to walk or jog with them daily, and so they are also kept fit. Moreover, pets not only fill many lonely hours for people who live alone or feel isolated from friends and family, but they are great ice-breakers, too. They encourage conversation with other pet owners which may lead to new friendships.

On the other hand, a large group of people is convinced that animals in home, despite its advantages, also exhibits several limitations, the most significant of which are that pets cost money and can hinder their owner from traveling if satisfactory pet-sitting arrangements are not available. From the point of view of those who are opposed to keeping pets, on the grounds that pets are dirty and there is always smell in the apartment, the pet owner is always responsible for the pet and must ensure the surroundings are kept clean by collecting and disposing of its animal's waste properly. However, the serious drawback in this remark is that it fails to take into consideration that proper training can help pets not be destructive or cause troubles.

Taking everything into account, it could be concluded that owning pets has both advantages and disadvantages too. Therefore, it would be wise to consider it from both sides, as well as our potential to satisfy the pet needs, before we decide to have one.

(Word Number: 392)

Topic Question: Human beings have kept animals since the earliest times. What are the benefits and disadvantages of pet ownership?

Keeping companion animals plays an important role to the life of their owner as these animals can form close bond with their owner. However, pet ownership is a far from black and white issue, so that it is worthwhile to investigate it from both sides as it has undoubtedly advantages as well as disadvantages, neither of which should be ignored.

To begin with, the most serious argument in favor of having a pet is that it reduces stress. In addition to this, they can help people keep healthy. As dogs need lots of exercise to keep fit and healthy, they force their owner to walk or jog with them daily, and so they are also kept fit. Moreover, pets let you make new friends. Instead of being alone or isolated from others, they act as ice-breakers and encourage conversation with other pet owners which may lead to new friendships.

The most serious disadvantages of having pets relates mostly to the responsibility of caring for them. Pet owners must ensure their animals get proper medical treatment, as well as the required vaccination. Nevertheless, pets may still be a health risk for some people. They can cause various illnesses to their owners, as, for example, many people have allergies to different animals. Therefore, families with allergy-prone members should reconsider about having pets.

Taking everything into account, it could be concluded that owning pets has both advantages and disadvantages too. Therefore, it would be wise to consider it from both sides, as well as our potential to satisfy the pet needs, before we decide to have one.

(Word Number: 264)

Part II

Topic Points

4. Technology

- Technological developments, the widespread use of the Internet and computer technology, **are rapidly changing/ has had a huge impact on** many aspects of our society
- Technology has brought about major changes in the business world, influencing the world of work, the way we work, and the jobs we do
- The work has been reduced. A great part of it is now done by computers, or robotic machines
- Familiarity with new technology (be computer literate and keep up with the latest computer programs) is necessary in order for the people to be employable
- There are fewer jobs for less-skilled workers
- More vacancies for highly skilled people are now available
- Many manual jobs almost disappeared
- Factories have become more automated
- Entirely new jobs are emerging, e.g. web designers and computer animators

- Technology has changed the kind of work many people can do
- Electronic communication has brought about enormous changes to the way business is conducted
- Information can now be transmitted quickly and easily via the Internet
- Communications technology enables business to be more flexible
- Video conferencing makes meetings between people in different locations possible

Pros/for/advantages/benefits/ positive results

- It boosts the economy
  - It creates new business and learning opportunities
  - It increases return on investment, as through the use of the Internet businesses can easily reach their target clients at a much reduced cost
  - It increased production and improved profit (increase efficiency and productivity)
  - Though technology is always expensive, it creates more profit
  - It improves the efficiency of delivery and distribution mechanisms

- o Significantly improves the efficiency and benefits of business across industries
  - o More job opportunities. It has created an immense amount of new jobs
  - o An entirely new group of people are needed to work with, develop, and maintain the new technology
  - o The work is more accurate and every product manufactured is the same.
  - o Communications technology enables business to be more flexible. For example, Video conferencing makes meetings between people in different locations possible.
  - o Decentralization: Technological innovations have lead business to be decentralized as companies move their headquarters from business capitals to towns were rent and salaries are lower
  - o The internet has given small companies and individuals access to the global market. Examples:
    - ✓ many companies advertise and accept orders on their own websites
    - ✓ Small tourist companies are less reliant on foreign travel agencies than they were in the past
  - o New business paths are emerging: in advertising, the media, web designers and computer animators
- It improves comfort and standard of living, e.g. it provides
  - o better housing
  - o the ability to keep food cold (refrigerators)
  - o better and more efficient heating of homes during winter
  - o cooling of homes during summer
  - o With a computer and internet connection one can even work without leaving home and going to the office
- It makes communication easier all over the globe (Better mass communication)
  - o Easier access to information without leaving our house (e.g. looking for a cure to headache, do shopping, writing an academic paper, search for a job, order food, book a vacation)
  - o Search engines, such as Google, enable us to access any form of information across all over the world
  - o Improved communication through internet and mobile phones allow us to talk to, video chat with, or collaborate with anybody in the entire world
  - o Through social networking (such as Facebook and Twitter) people from all over the world have been brought even closer
  - o We can get in touch with friends and family from just about any corner of the world
  - o Electronic communication (e.g. email) makes sharing information with a large group of people easy
  - o Email has made communication, especially abroad, much simpler and faster, resulting in numerous benefits for commerce and business
  - o Using the World Wide Web information on every conceivable subject is now available to everyone
  - o Almost any person has access to news, medical advice, online education courses via the internet

- o Staying in contact is easier now than it has ever been
- Incredible medical care: Technology improves medical care/ healthcare and enhances the longevity.
  - o Surgical procedures and every day functions have been made simpler and more efficient
  - o Organ transplant is more successful now than in the past
- It assists scientific research and consequent supports the advancement of human knowledge (e.g. Space exploration), and provides us with deeper insights.
  - o It makes research, purchasing, or discovering new things simpler
  - o In an earlier time finding information required visiting to the library or owning an encyclopedia
  - o Today, data access is possible from everywhere and almost at any time
  - o Encourages innovation and creativity
  - o There are massive amounts of data that can be mined for numerous insights and benefits
  - o Convenience in education through the creation and use of appropriate platforms to access technology and knowledge
  - o Do not have to go to class to access education, the same is provided online
- It allows us to experience new cultures.
  - o Provides better understanding of others cultures
  - o Has made the planet a smaller place
  - o Provides convenience of travelling through airplanes and trains
  - o Makes possible to travel to the other places of the world, to see new countries, new cultures, new opportunities, over a very short time
  - o It can be used to improve our ability to preserve, protect and restore ancient heritage (buildings or pieces of art e.g. paintings) *so that they can be enjoyed and understood by future generations*
- It saves time and energy and allows us to do more with less
  - o Things can be done almost instantly with the use of technology
  - o More work in less time can be done
  - o Computers can work with greater efficiency when compared to human
  - o Faster and improved communication, manufacturing processes, and automated systems
  - o Delivery of merchandises can be done on time through advanced forms of transport
  - o The technological advance has made life far easier and more convenient for large numbers of people

Cons/against/disadvantages/ negative results/problems

Environment
- Plants may pollute water resources on various levels
- Toxic fumes are released into the air as a byproduct of converting fuel into energy

- The chemicals we use for cleaning, and wastes from factories go into our water systems and pollute the water we drink and the fish we eat
- Some of the pesticides we have sprayed on our crops have been found to be dangerous, and this kind of pollution may stay in the ground for a very long period of time
- Pollution caused by chemicals destroys the ozone layer. Aerosol cans, refrigeration and air conditioning systems emit chemicals which break down the stratospheric ozone (ozone layer). Without ozone, not only human beings but also all plant and animal life are exposed to dangerous radiation from sun
- Emissions of certain gasses, mostly carbon dioxide and methane, increase the warming of the earth's atmosphere, leading to the melting of the polar ice caps, and the raising of the sea level. As a consequence, many parts of the world would be submerged below the sea level

Internet
- It is nearly impossible to regulate and control the Web due to its large size
- Children can access unsuitable websites
- Hackers can use the internet to steal personal information
- It has given birth to weapons of mass destruction
  - The misuse of technology has lead to the creation of conventional, chemical, biological and nuclear weapons
- Moral and spiritual values are being destroyed and replaced by other values based on the chase of profit and the individual wellbeing
- Technology is not cheap as
  - certain socioeconomic groups do not have any access to new technologies because of their cost, even for technologies that are considered to be essential to life, such as medical advances and health care (standard vaccines)
  - it has been developed based on the idea that everything is a profit/loss concept
- Makes people, businesses, and activities quickly obsolete, and creates the need to constantly upgrade
  - The newest and best piece of technology, will become obsolete in very little time
  - The more that technology advances, the faster new and more efficient versions are designed
  - Landfills are filled up with no longer used computers, cell phones, and other things that are damaging to the environment
- Creates a generation of laziness
  - It makes some people more lazy, especially those who use electronic communication to interact with each other while being in the same room, displaying a lazy behavior
  - When everything is made easier, or completely done for us through the use of technology, people (especially children) are getting accustomed to not do anything
- Fewer job opportunities/ Loss of employment

o There are fewer employment opportunities because most of the work is done by the machines and the robots
o Robots are slowly replacing humans in the workplace
o Robots can literally perform most of the functions that were previously performed by man
o No need left for humans to work as robots work in a more efficient manner and produce greater results
o Factories have become more automated which have as consequence fewer jobs for less-skilled workers and more for highly skilled people
o People need to be more familiar with new technology in order to be employable
o Office workers need to be computer literate and keep up with the latest computer programs
o Many manual jobs almost disappeared
- It has negative effects on individuals
  o Intensive computer use may lead to health problems such as hand, wrist, and forearm pain, obesity, tendonitis
  o It may lead to social isolation, lack of human contact, depression, inactivity, addiction, especially among the youth who spend most of their time in social networking sites
  o There is the threat of loss of human touch in nearly all aspects of human life
  o Lack of understanding among individuals due to the lack of face to face conversation
  o Reduced/Lack of privacy
  o The internet enables almost anyone to find out a lot of personal information about someone else
  o Cameras in most public locations make it possible to track a person's every movement online and in real life

4.2. Computers/Information Technology (IT)

Computers have made a very vital impact on society having changed the way of life as their use has affected every field of it, medicine, business, industry, airline and weather forecasting, to name only a few.

- Computers have entered into almost every area of our life
- In the future there will be few aspects of our life that will not be influenced by computers
- In the future, computers (using for instance video-conferencing platforms) will probably
  o control more and more forms of communication
  o transform education and business

- Without computers life would have certain difficulties
- Their speed and memory save us a great deal of time and space
- The Internet has completely changed the way we communicate with **one another/other people**
- The Internet gives us access to a mine of information at the touch of a button
- The use of computers makes work processes (different tasks) faster, easier, far more efficient, and less prone to errors
- They save up time and effort and reduces the overall cost to complete a particular task by
  - keeping the records of customers
  - maintaining accounts
  - managing financial transactions
  - online banking (checking account balance and making financial transaction from everywhere using the internet)
  - The transactions are handled easily and quickly with computerized systems
- People are using computers for
  - paying their bills
  - managing their home budgets
  - having some break and watching a movie
  - listening to songs
  - playing computer games
- Online services like Skype or social media websites are used for communication and information sharing purposes
- Are a powerful instrument of calculation, as they can perform almost all kinds of computations, releasing us from the tiresome, repetitive calculation work
  - Scientists can do special research which could never be done in the past
  - Engineers can deal with complex problems in engineering within a short time, which perhaps would take years to solve without the computer
  - Help the work of the accountant to calculate the production costs and to distribute employees' salaries
  - From space travel to bacteria research, from central government planning to the modern family affairs, the computer can make a significant contribution
- Promotes progress, such as
  - Information processing: especially in the area of information collection and processing, which is different from what we had in the past
  - In medical research: was it not for them the cure for many deadly diseases would not have been discovered
- Computers and IT (Information Technology), in general, are invaluable in physics, chemistry and biology: numerous experiments are currently being carried out
- Far more efficient method of storage of a vast amount of information providing easier access to stored information (computer search engines)

- It is a perfect communication device that has brought human beings many benefits
- They allow and encourage the free exchange of information on a global basis
- Allow the dissemination of news and opinion via the internet

- Improper and prolonged use of computer entails health risks as it can result in injuries or disorders of hands, wrists, elbows, eyes, necks and back
- Using a personal computer too much can have negative effects on our health
- By staring at a screen for too long we can put our eyes under stress
- Sitting in the same position for hours is not the best way to treat our body
- Avoiding these health risks requires using the computer in proper position, taking regular breaks while using the computer for longer period of time, e.g. a couple of minutes break after 30 minutes of computer usage.
- We have become more and more dependent on computers
- People, mostly young people, have grown so fond of technology and gadgets, and have become too dependent on computers
- As society depends more and more on computers, many people become excluded or fall victim to new technology since many jobs require at least a basic knowledge of computers
- Different tasks are performed automatically by computers reducing the need of people and increasing unemployment rate in society
- Some people cannot afford a computer
- Others have no experience when they need to use one
- If people rely too much on computers for communication, they may begin to communicate less and less face to face or verbally
- The internet has become a forum for illicit material including pornography, advice on how to construct explosive devices at home and so on
- Criminal activities are made possible, such as withdrawing someone else's money from the bank.
- Computers can be overused, even addictively, and lead to waste of time and energy
  - Many people, especially the young generation, use computers pointlessly by playing games, spend a great deal of time on the social media websites, chatting for long periods of time, or texting their friends all night through smart phones
  - It causes them to waste their time and energy, affecting their study, their health, and their social life
  - Even normal communication between friends and family can suffer
- Computers have created serious Data Security problems, as the data stored on a computer connected to the internet can be accessed by unauthorized persons through network programs

- Some people use the computer and the network for committing crimes, electronic or computer crimes
  - They can hack the credit card numbers of others and misuse them
  - They can steal important data from big organizations
- As the computers are used from companies all over the world to store personal data of the people, the privacy of a person can easily be violated if the personal and confidential records are not protected properly

4.3. Technology in the Classroom

Pros/for/advantages/benefits/ positive results

- It allows teachers to experiment more in different pedagogy methods and get instant feedback
  - allows for more active learning
  - increases engagement through multimedia quiz questions during lectures (with instantaneous results)
  - enhances teaching by embedding links to subject relevant materials
- Ensure full participation by engaging all students, including shy students who would not normally raise their hand in class
- Teachers can easily and regularly have feedback on assignments and adjust the coursework accordingly
- There are many online resources (scientific and educational apps and platforms, e-textbooks) that can enhance the education and make the learning process more fun and effective
- Computers can help automate tedious and time-consuming tasks, as keeping track of student attendance and performance, providing more space for effective teaching and learning
- Computer can be used as a great educational tool
  - Students can have instant access to **all sort of/the newest** information on the internet (up to date textbooks and course materials) that can supplement their learning experience
  - Some websites provides free resources for students and professionals
  - Calculations or printing are easier and faster
- Students can networked together online, share information, work together on group projects, and interact with the instructor, fostering a more collaborative learning environment
- Student become digitally literate
  - They get a deeper understanding of the digital world
  - They become able to intuitively adapt new contexts and co-create content with others
  - They learn to differentiate reliable from unreliable sources on the Internet
- Information Technology reduces the amount of text books students must carry to school

- Visual illustrations on computers make learning easier
- Learning can be enhanced through videos from the Internet, or using puzzles academic games to solve specific challenges while in the classroom

Cons/against/disadvantages/ negative results/problems

- Can be distracting from learning (computers, laptops, or tablets), both for users and for those around them
  - Students learn less when during lectures
  - Students tend to earn worse grades
- Information Technology changes how students socially interact with one another
- Information Technology can disconnect students from social interactions affecting their ability to verbally communicate
- Information Technology could encourage/foster cheating in the classroom and on assignments, as it can facilitate this process
- Information Technology creates socioeconomic separations in the classroom
  - Not all students have equal access to technological resources, or can afford the equipment required in class
  - Computers are expensive, so not every school or student is able to afford a computer of their own in the classroom
  - In most cases, a group of students shares one computer
- Students need guidance on proper and beneficial use of the Internet
  - The quality of research and information they find may be controversial
  - Not all online sources are proper and unreliable
  - They must be able to identify them

4.4.Internet shopping/on-line shopping
Pros/ for/ advantages/benefits

- Convenience. It is quick and easy as can be done from anywhere with an internet connection at any time of the day with a simple click of a mouse
- Infinite choice. Vast array of products, including those from other countries, are made readily available
- Good discounts and lower prices
- Products sold online are often cheaper than those sold in stores
- Many online stores sell products at really low prices because of the lack of money spent on overheads
- Traditional stores have operating costs: rent, staffing, water, heat that affects the products prices
- Online shopping is an invaluable way to save money as online stores are highly competitive with other online and traditional stores

- Price comparisons. Search engines make finding and comparing prices for products easy
- Easy access to consumer reviews. Price-comparison websites make deal hunting easier and can guide shoppers to stores with the best offer and reputation, by posting reviews submitted
- Online stores never close, there are no annoying crowds, and online shoppers do not have to wait in long queues to check out
- No pressure sales. There are rarely aggressive or eager salespeople to deal with

Cons/ against/ disadvantages

- There are more deceptive offers in online stores and sometimes a deal that looks great falls short of what has been advertised
- Advertised free products may sometimes be charged with the cost of shipping so that they are not really free for the shopper, and maybe even provide profit from the purchase
- Websites attractiveness encourage spending which can lead to over-spending and even addiction
- Delivery charges and/or shipping insurance often apply, making products more expensive than they seem to be
- There may be shipping costs or delays and no guarantee of delivery
- Delivery can be slow and sometimes unreliable
- Risk of products lost during shipment is present
- Credit card fraud risk is possible
- You cannot try things on. There is no any ability to physically inspect or try on the items being considered for purchase
- You cannot try on clothes, check the material, see the design from close, or get the product immediately after you pay
- There is no any possibility to negotiate the price and the payment terms, as it may be the case in local stores
- When there is a problem, solving it face-to-face with local store employees may be faster and more satisfying than in online stores
- Quality issues. It is easier to drop off a faulty item back to your local store than to an online store

4.5. Internet/social networks/media

Pros/for/ advantages/benefits

- It has increased/fostered communication between people and countries across the globe (world)
- It enhances communication, availability of information and makes file sharing easier

- Has brought people closer together than ever before making worldwide communication possible
- It provides ways of communication that were impossible in the past
- Instant messaging allows users to talk in real time and send files to others
- It allows access to a vast amount of useful information
- It facilitates quick and inexpensive communication via emails, video calls or social networks
- E-mail has made communication much simpler and faster resulting in numerous benefits for commerce and business
- E-mail and social networking sites have created online communities that are global in scale
- It allows us to find and rediscover long-lost school friends
- Creates an environment that allows us to interact easily with others: we can share our photos, videos, links and thoughts with our friends
- It allows people to maintain and enrich friendships
- It is a tool that allows us to stay more deeply connected with a larger and more diverse set of friends
- **Contradiction of the past**:
  - communication was only possible by phone or mail, which entailed time and expense
  - kept in contact only with those people already known to you
- It has take people closer to each other independent from where they are, improving communication
- It allows people to keep abreast of current events (news, medical advice, ancient history, online education courses)
- Large companies can share resource with their employees and customers conveniently

Cons/ against/ disadvantages

- The widespread use of email destroys traditional forms of communication such as letter writing, telephone and face-to-face conversation. **Result**: decline in people's basic ability to socialize and interact with each other on a day-to-day basis
- Users can get addicted to it and lose touch with reality due to the allure of the virtual world
- People, especially the younger generation, spend hours of their time online chatting, which is certainly not the same as the real interaction with humans
- Many children are getting caught up in online games staying at home glued to the screen instead of interacting with their peer
- Feelings of isolation are arisen for those individuals who do not have a 'real' person to turn to in times of need

- The large size of the web has made it nearly impossible to be regulated and controlled. **Result**: Concerns have been raised regarding children accessing unsuitable websites and viruses.
- It is easier for the children to access potentially dangerous sites, such as pornography sites, as they can register claiming to be an adult
- There is a large possibility of identity theft. **Result**: invasion of the privacy of the individual.
- Possibility of getting computer viruses
- Hence the demand of computer viruses and malware is increased
- Only the rich can afford access to the internet
- It requires an efficient handler since computing skills are necessary to operate the internet, so new technology gap develops
- The Internet has led to radical changes to the way that people consume and share information

Solution

- Adequate legislation and controls have to be established preventing young people from accessing dangerous sites
- Parents need to closely monitor their children' activities and restrict their access to certain sites
- Various computer programs provide control of the websites children can access
- Companies must improve their security systems to hinder fraud and hacking making them more difficult

4.6. Popularity of social networks

Reasons

- They are free of charge and accessible to almost everyone regardless of economic status, unless they have a computer and an Internet access
- Give users a strong sense of belonging to a community
- Users can log on and instantly connect to their group of friends
- Give people the option of making new friends by choosing from a large number member profiles

Effects/results

- Many people, as well as communities, are no more isolated from the rest of the world
- Social Networks have opened a window on the world giving people deeper insight into global events and different mentalities
- Social Networks have promoted the mass culture

- Communities sometimes lose their unique cultural identity
- Many otherwise active, sociable and extroverted people end up adopting a sedentary lifestyle, spending hours at home glued to a screen

4.7. Mobile phones

Pros/for/ advantages/benefits

- Cell/Mobile phones are small, portable, and transportable providing a high level of portability
- You can go across the countries with little worry of losing communication service
- Smart phones allow users to connect to the internet without a computer, having no difficulty with searching for data, using social media, helping with study, or finding the right directions to go
- Cell phones also facilitate communication among family members and friends
- Mobile phones allow people to get connected with emergency services, family, or friends in case of emergency
- They facilitate constant communication between parents and children, allowing parents to stay in touch with their children
- Parents have not to worry about where their children are because they can always reach them by their cell phone
- If children need to stay after school or need a ride, they will be able to call their parents to let them know
- Cell phones are important in emergency situations, when for instance parents need to quickly get in touch with their children or vice versa
- Cell phones provide a sense of security in cases you get lost, your car breaks down, or even if you feel threatened while walking through a poorly lit area
- They have a plethora of tools that can be very handy. In fact, they are all-in-one device, mp3 player, digital camera, phone, GPS, e-book reader, and gaming device, all in your pockets at the same time, and comfortably
- Cell phones can be a powerful learning tool. Their technical features and applications enable children to learn a lot of things using them
- With Mobile phones, pictures can be taken instantly, quickly and conveniently, sent out and deleted, saving time and money, without the need of another device, such as a photo or video camera
- Cell phones have made (business) communication much easier and much more convenient
- Business people are no longer tied to their offices, they can make and receive business calls from any place
- Cell phones make it easy to keep in touch with your beloved who are traveling or live far away

- Cell phones can be used to cheat in exams in schools, if they are allowed to be used
- Mobile phones, especially smart phones, are really expensive to purchase
- Texting or calling while driving may cause traffic accidents
- They become out of fashion very quickly, as almost everyone wishes to have the newest, fastest and fanciest cell phone on the market. In addition, applications' upgrades make cell phones obsolete
- Cell phone contain elements that may pollute the environment if discarded in landfills and not treated properly (electronic-waste recycling)
- Cell phones can be very distracting, especially as far as they concern children, diverting them from important tasks they should do, such as studying, doing homework or even crossing the street
- Many people are addicted to their mobile phones and even the idea of leaving them at home or turning them off would give them instant anxiety
- Many people are obsessed with checking in on Facebook, Instagram, Twitter and other social media networks and use their smart phones for this purpose
- Smart phones can be used to send sexual messages or pictures to other persons very easy blackmailing them or requiring money, or forcing them to sex exploitation
- Smart phones offer Internet access, giving child the opportunity to visit websites and use social media that may not normally be allowed to access
- The monthly cell phone bill can be a large expense in the household budget

Solution

- Since they can be connected to the internet easy, they would be taken away from children while they are studying.

4.8. Banning Cell phones in Schools

- Classroom should be a cell phone-free area
- Cell phones should at least be switched off in class

Pros/for/advantages/ benefits

- Teenagers do not seem to be able to give up their cell phones
- Cell phone activity disrupts the lessons and makes keeping order in the classroom even more difficult for the teacher
- Cell phones are often used at the wrong times and in the wrong places
- Students use them to send messages to their friends during lessons
- Teenagers use their cell phones to listen to music, take photos and videos, play games, and send messages during the class time

- Teens are constantly busy with their cell phones in the classroom and cannot be concentrated on the lesson

Cons/against/disadvantages

- Cell phones are a part of life today
- Cell phones are very popular today and have become a necessity for teens
- Students need cell phones to keep in contact with their parents during the day and after school. If they are going to be late or early, they need to be able to contact their parents, so they must be able to use their cell phone to call their parents and let them know
- Teens today have so many after-school activities and they often need to be picked up or driven somewhere, so they need their cell phones to arrange for their parents to pick them up after school
- There are many dangers in society today. Having a cell phone allows teens to call the police or their parents **for help/ to get help** in case of emergency
- Parents can be in contact with their children at any moment with the cell phone

4.9. Television

There are concerns **about/regarding** the television programs children are watching (children television viewing choices)

Pros/for/ advantages/benefits

- Television is a cheap and easy source of entertainment, information and education
- It provides access to international news, making it easy to stay informed about world news
- It can keep us up to date with world events and developments
- It offers on the spot reports/coverage
- There are channels that are exclusively educational increasing our knowledge
- There are channels that provide access to information on many subjects, such as cooking, home improvement, investing, and so much more
- It can be used to learn a foreign language
- Television can make people feel less lonely
- Television events can be seen as gathering opportunities for families and friends
- There are TV Programs for younger children that teach them the basics of reading and math in an engaging manner giving them the needed repetition that aids in retention
- Historical movies, nature programs and documentaries can all be extremely informative
- Television can help children to experience the world on a widescreen through visual effects

- Quiz shows and certain cartoons can provide free and harmless entertainment
- Television has allowed the whole of society access cultural entertainment
- With the television it is now possible for everyone to enjoy, for example, watch ballet and theatre
- We can learn more about other cultures and societies by watching interesting documentaries about them on television
- Television helps people to expand their minds through
  - watching others travels
  - being taught about different cultures and societies,
  - giving people a broader understanding of the world that we and other people live in

- Many TV programs contain unsuitable content
- The violence, crime, and sex often depicted on many Television shows, programs and movies can have negative impacts on young, especially, impressionable children
- Kids that are frequently exposed to TV violence may more likely reenact this violent and aggressive behavior
- Watching too much television may harm our health causing health issues, behavior problems, sleep difficulties, make people antisocial, waste time, and, as far as students are concerned, result in lower grades
- Television advertisements may be brainwashing and lead people into consumerism
- Television has been seen as a potential cause of making people shallow, because of the poor content of the majority of the TV programs and shows
- Many TV programs do not go into important and crucial details about several issues, or they intentionally present them in a biased **way/view**
- Too much television can ruin human relationships, especially if someone is spending excessive time watching TV, and not enough time interacting with the persons they love
- Television can be addictive resulting in spending more and more time watching almost any TV program, show or movie, which is hard to stop
- Students who watch a lot of TV
  - get poor grades
  - are not as interested in social or sport activities
  - have a more negative outlook on life
- Certain movies show violent scenes which encourage aggressive behavior
- Daytime soap operas can portray an unrealistic view of life
- Watching too much television passively can inhibit imagination because children do not have to think for themselves, instead, they watch things passively
- Violent media accustoms viewers to cruelty

- TV use by children should be closely monitored by their parents
- Parents should pay close attention to the types of programs their children are watching
- Parents should take the opportunity/time to
    - watch television with their children and discuss the content of the programs they like watching
    - listen to their children express their opinions as frequent as possible
    - read the TV guide together with their children
    - discuss which show sends positive messages and point out which ones do not
    - help children choose television programs that are suitable for their age
    - teach children to determine if a show is age-appropriate and explain why
    - discuss programs and study the contents of the TV guide beforehand
    - explain their feelings about the TV shows and programs and point out the things they object to
- Parents should build trust with their children and their decisions regarding which programs to watch

Results

As parents cannot always be present, these actions can bring positive results:

- Children will gradually become able to develop their own understanding of which program is acceptable to watch and which is not
- Soon enough, children will become responsible television viewers

4.10. Education and Technology

Pros/for/ advantages/benefits

- Technology offers the flexibility to educate people with a variety of different means
- The lecturer and tutor are able to use interactive tools to deliver their courses in a large numbers of students been located anywhere
- It is now no longer essential for students to be present in the lecture theatre for their courses (distance learning)
- Distance learning courses for adults who are in employment and/or in other countries are available

- Despite the fact that they are part of the digital generation, not all students are comfortable with using technology, and they may suffer from their lack of technological skills
- Education is a activity that works best with as much human interaction as possible
- Technology cannot replace the human contact found in traditional face-to-face tutorials and seminars

4.11. Genetic Engineering/ Research/Cloning

Pros/for/ advantages/benefits

- Genetic engineering in humans is the answer to the multitude of problems that millions face today
- Gene therapy can be used to treat inherited genetic defects by removing a faulty gene and replacing it with a functioning gene in cells lacking malfunctions
- Hereditary baldness, heart problems, mental disorders, and many genetic diseases would cease to exist
- It may lead to a cure for several diseases such as cancer
- We can cope with illnesses that have no cure or treatment, or that have long and painful treatments and are applied with difficulty. **Example**: treatment of leukemi4. Patients suffering from leukemia can be cured only if another person has been found whose tissues match those of the patient, with very low probability, even for identical twins
- It may result in the creation of replacement organs in the laboratory instead of relying on donors for organ transplants
- Cloning can helps in organ replacement
- Cloning animals and organs is useful for the improvement of quality of human life and for the treatment of lethal diseases (organ transplantation)
- Alteration of pig DNA to suit human immunology may resolve organ donor shortage
    - o Pig organs function in similar ways and have a similar size to human organs
    - o Pig immunology is similar to that of humans but the problem of organ rejection still remains
- Genetic Engineering will benefit mankind medically, industrially, and agriculturally
- There could be an abundance of donor organs without the wait
- It could also create new medicine for diseases untreatable before
- Cloning animals enables developments in science
- Through Genetic Engineering of animals, a large amount of proteins can be produced

- Farmyard animals (cows, goats) could produce milk that could be altered and used as a medicine
- It could create natural fertilizers
- It enables the researchers to create organisms with genes that they normally would not have and study them
- Genetically enhanced superior food products can be produced

- Genetic engineering and cloning holds the potential to
  - solve several humankind problems
  - to develop unchecked dangers
- Genetic engineering raises a lot of moral and ethical questions
- Is it unethical and immoral humans "playing god"
- It is morally wrong to tamper with nature
- It is unethical to show a disease before the symptoms appear
- Using genetic engineering to predict genetic diseases causes controversy since there are bioethics issues predicting untreatable inherited illnesses
- Manipulation of nature may have unforeseen consequences which are irreversible and may have adverse effects on ecosystems
- It can pose a serious threat to the existence of life on earth
- Once started the genetically alteration of living systems, then may not be easy to put a stop
- Genetic engineering may create organisms that human beings will not have defense against
- Genetic engineering may result in genetic defects, as gene therapy in humans can have various unknown side effects
- Attempting to treat one defect with genetic therapy may result in another
- It creates a high risk to disturb the balance of Nature
- Genetically altered plants can grow in places they were not planted
- Some genetic modifications can create species, animals or plants, that can have strange effects on ecosystems
- Some genetically altered crops might cause serious allergic reactions if ingested by humans due to the production of certain proteins with adverse effects on humans organism
- There may be an imbalance in the fertility of soil and the growth of the wildlife, farm animals, and human beings
- It can lead to serious species deformities in growth, development and health, as there are many disorders known due to the mutation of a single gene
- There is the risk of accidentally release of harmful organisms, as well as deliberate release of organisms such as bacterial pesticides
- The survival, growth, and distribution of genetically modified bacteria may have long-term harmful ecological results that cannot be effectively predicted

- Disease-producing organisms used in food products might develop worldwide epidemics
- Any type of genetically engineered animal is hazardous to the environment
- There is always the dangerous risk of all new advances: their undeniable potential for biological warfare
  - More resistant infections or diseases spread in the enemy's area scare all people
  - Pathogens could spread to the enemies livestock or crops, resulting in starvation of a whole nation and into surrender

Pros/for/ advantages/benefits

- Genetic engineering may allow the creation of crops that
  - are disease resistant
  - are pesticide resistant
  - may lead to a decrease in the use of chemical pesticides and insecticides
- It can lead to crop abundance, increasing crop yield
- Plants produced genetically modified may be able to grow in any type of soil
- Farmers may have financial gain due to increased crop yields and efficiency
- It may lead to increased nutritional value of crops and of improved flavor
- It can offer better quality, longer shelf life of products, more uniformity of crops and more efficient harvesting
- Food production costs can be lowered and health, taste and look of a product maximized
- Food shortage problems in the Third World could be solved by adapting crops to grow in harsh conditions
- Genetic engineering can serve in the production of adequate quantities of food and solve the human problem many people face in the third world countries: suffering from malnutrition and hunger
- May lead to better growth rate, taste and nutrition of crops like tomatoes, potatoes, rice and soybean
- Genetically engineering can produce new variants of common species with increased yield and improved nutritional qualities
- Genetically engineered crops can survive on lands that are currently not suited for cultivation
- Genetic manipulation can be carried out to improve/meliorate the nutritional value and the taste of food and increase the rate of growth of certain crops
- Genetic engineering produces crops which are pest-resistant and have a longer shelf life

- Engineered seeds can endure harsh climatic and soil conditions and are resistant to pests
- Genetic engineering may be utilized to slow down food spoilage process, resulting in greater shelf life of vegetables and fruits

- The created "super crops" are genetically similar to the natural and therefore they are also prone to pests, insect attacks or diseases
- Genetically modified crops may threaten biodiversity by decreasing richness and variety of species
- The nutritional value of genetically modified food is questionable
- There are concerns about the safety of these products
- Labeling genetically modified products is inefficient and sometimes misleading because the initial modifying materials are not listed
- Some people may have allergic reaction because of proteins normally not found in natural products
- Ingredients contained in genetically modified food may react with the human body in negative ways increasing the risk to human health by causing cancer and other diseases
- Genetic Engineering
    - may impede food nutritional value
    - contaminates crop genes
    - may lead to unwanted genetic mutations resulting in food allergies
    - may introduce harmful pathogens
    - bring about new pathogens
    - by raising the plant's immunity to present diseases, may result in transferring the resistant genetically added or modifies genes to harmful pathogens with unforeseeable consequences
- Crops genetically engineered may take the place of natural weeds and harm natural species
- Genetic engineering is detrimental to genetic diversity

4.13. Organic versus Conventionally Produced Food

- Organic food does not contain any kind of poisons or additives
- It is clean and fresh and good for our health
- Organic food is produced in harmony with the environment
- Organic farming methods help build up healthy soil and use natural controls for insects and weeds

Organic Food Cons/Disadvantages

- Organic food can be expensive, it costs more than conventionally produced food, but considering its benefits, it is well worth the price

Conventionally Produced Food Cons/Disadvantages

- Conventionally produced food has many additives
- Fruits and vegetables are grown with the use of pesticides and herbicides
- Cows on conventional farms are fed hormones and antibiotics
- The pesticides and herbicides that are used with conventionally produced food poison the environment as well as our bodies
- These are poisonous substances that stay on our food, and we ingest them when we eat these products
- Over the years, this can cause serious health problems such as cancer
- Chemicals can harm insects and other animals and deplete the soil of nutrients

5. Teenage Problems

5.1. Sitting Exams

Problems caused by sitting exams

- Exam time brings with it extra stresses and pressures to the students. The pressure of expectation, exam results, and decisions for the future, and the insecurity about it
- A bit of stress for a short period of time can be productive as it can motivate students to perform at their best
- Excessive stress causes teen to be unable to study and in need of some extra support
- When children and young people experience stress, they may:
  - worry a lot and feel tense
  - get lots of headaches and stomach pains
  - not sleep well
  - be irritable
  - lose interest in food or eat more than normal
  - do not enjoy activities they previously enjoyed
  - seem negative and low in their mood
  - seem hopeless about the future

Solutions. Exam revision Tips

- Students should
  - take breaks, or arrange some downtime, as necessarily as possible so they can have a break from revision for the exams, and to avoid, or relief, lost temper and moodiness
  - be calm, positive and reassuring and put the whole thing into perspective
  - get ready for exams with plenty of planning
  - establish a revision routine by re-arranging their schedules and priorities with the most suitable manner that works for them
  - prepare a checklist to make sure they have studied everything they should
- Parents should be flexible **during exams/ around exam time**. They should
  - keep TV and music volumes down while their children are studying
  - make sure that their children have a quiet and comfortable place to work and study
  - If there is not any a suitable spot at home, they should make it easy for their children to study elsewhere, like in the library

- o better go out and let their children have the house to themselves at crucial times for a adequately amount of time
- o be tolerant (lenient) about chores and untidiness as much as it is possible
- o remind their child that feeling anxious and nervous is normal, as nervousness is a natural reaction to exams
- o encourage teen to go to sleep at a reasonable time
- o make sure their child eats well, have healthy meals and don't drink too much caffeine, as a balanced diet is vital for their health, and can help them to feel well during exams
- o arrange for their children a healthy and nutritious breakfast to help them focus and concentrate on the exam process
- o try to reduce teen's stress by making sure they take regular breaks
- o try to discuss any expectation, decision, and insecurity about their future the teens may have
- o try to avoid nagging them as it causes them lose their focus
- o give their child lots of encouragement so they feel more positive before they leave for the exams

5.2. Bullying at School

Forms

Bullying at school takes many forms. Some of them are:
- physical (hitting, shoving, kicking, destroying or stealing property, or threats of violence)
- verbal (name-calling, insulting, threatening to physically harm, mocking, intimidating, harassing, taunting, spreading rumors, making racist remarks and sexist comments)
- relational aggression (excluding other teens from their company, talking behind another person's back, spreading rumors and lies, and participating in gossip)
- sexual (humiliating words and actions that target a person sexually, slut shaming, making crude comments, vulgar gestures, propositioning, uninvited touching, exposure to pornographic materials, sexual name-calling, and spreading rumors about another person's sexual activity)
- cyber bullying (technology use – cell phones, instant messaging, YouTube, social networking, e-mail, chat rooms, blogs – as a way to engage in relational aggression and verbal bullying)

- Bullying differs from mean behavior as bullies intend to harm their targets. It is not a one-time act but an ongoing pattern of behavior that is usually repeated.
- Cyber bullying can take place 24 hours a day, seven days a week, and, at times, it can be done anonymously. It is very attractive to bullies who will remain anonymous and physically removed from their targets. In most cases, sexual

bullying involves boys bullying girls, or girls bullying other girls, and in rare cases, girls bullying boys.

The motivations behind harmful bullying behavior are not easy to pinpoint. Some teens bully their peers in order to
- feel powerful and in control
- cope with unhappiness or anger
- react to others peer pressure
- deal with self-esteem and confidence issues
- or because they have little empathy for others

- Bullying turns school, what should be a place of learning, into a place of misery and even danger
- Relational aggression deprives teens of the opportunity to form meaningful connections with their peers
- When there is an imbalance of power, physical (the bully is older, larger, or stronger, or there is a gang of bullies targeting the victim) or psychological (the bullies have a higher social status, a sharper tongue, or more influence at school), it is hard for the target to defend themselves against the bully's attacks, and as a result the target of the bullying feels weak, oppressed, threatened, and vulnerable
- Teens being bullied
  - feel alone, helpless, unsafe, afraid, guilty, stressed, anxious, depressed, sad or down
  - often blame themselves for the bullying
  - have thoughts about suicide or hurting themselves
  - have trouble with their schoolwork
  - have problems with mood, energy level, sleep, and appetite
  - are nervous about going to school because they know they will face a bully who will pick on them
  - experience shame or fear and do not want to involve a parent or teacher
  - may lead to depression, drug use and stunted social development
  - may have physical problems and injuries as a result of physical bullying
  - may become violent, turning on their classmates in order to get revenge, retaliation

- Most kids do not readily talk about bullying. Instead, they keep the details to themselves and try to handle it on their own. Hence, because bullying does not go away on its own and it does not make a person stronger,
- Parents should

- o   build a strong relationship with their teenager children, as it is vital in helping them overcome bullying
  - o   make sure their children are physically safe and provide unconditional support
  - o   actively listen and focus on letting bullied teens know that it is not their fault
  - o   take steps to bring bullying to an end
  - o   encourage teens to talk to their school counselor
  - o   alert other personnel at the school which can help implement practical steps like changing the seating plan
- Teens
  - o   can talk to a trusted adult in positions of authority, such as parents, teachers, or coaches. They often can deal with bullying without the bully ever learning how they found out about it
  - o   can talk about it to a friend who can give the support they need
  - o   could use body language to send the message that they are not vulnerable: Walk tall and hold their head high
  - o   can ignore the bully and walk away, implying that they do not care, since bullies like getting a reaction
  - o   should practice confidence in order to be able to respond to the bully verbally or through their behavior
  - o   could have teachers and other adult authorities present when possible to discourage bullying behavior
  - o   could try to move in groups if possible, since bullies most often single out those who are alone
  - o   should seek friends who are supportive and kind
  - o   should not try to resolve the problem by resorting to physical violence, it is more likely to get hurt and into trouble if trying to fight a bully
  - o   should stand up for friends and other peers you see being bullied so as to help the victims feel supported and may stop the bullying

5.3. Changing schools

Results/Problems caused

- Disruption to any part of a teenager's life is likely to affect their education and emotional well-being

Reasons

- Children and teens need routine and structure in their daily lives, as it keeps them calm
- It is a huge change and a milestone event in children' life, let alone for the teens

- Students should try to turn anxiety into excitement, in order to enjoy the anticipation of starting at a new school
- Students should instead of imagining what can go wrong, create exciting images and imagine what can go right
- Students should talk things over with older siblings, cousins or friends who have recently changed schools to see what it was like
- Students should try to find out which of their friends may also be moving to the same place and agree to be allies and look after each other while things are new
- Students should learn to accept changes as a part of life as everything else, instead of seeing a big change as a scary thing
- Children could stay in touch with their friends of the old school after they leave
- Parent should involve their child in the decision over which school they attends
- Parent should prepare their child for the change and find out whether there are other children moving to the same school
- Parent should remain calm and cheerful because their anxiety may increase their child's anxiety
- Parents and kids could visit the school together to meet teachers before the first day, so that they can get familiar with it
- After moving schools, parents should try to make time to help their child settle in, since children' needs might not be so easy to be satisfied quickly, and friendships left behind cannot be replaced easily

5.4. Moving House

Results/Problems caused

- Disruption to any part of a teenager's life is likely to affect their education and emotional well-being

Reasons

- Teens need routine and structure in their daily lives, as it keeps them calm
- It is a huge life change and a milestone event in anyone's life, let alone for the teens

Solutions

When parents are thinking about moving, they should
- discuss the possibility with their children. Teens appreciate being part of the decision-making process, or at least being made to feel like they are
- list the positive aspects of this relocation, e.g. a cinema nearby or perhaps they will have a bigger bedroom at the new place

- offer teens as much reassurance as possible
- not move in their teenager mid-year, if it can be avoided
- remind teens of all things that are not going to change and allow them to share their worries and concerns with their parents
- take their children with them, when are looking at houses, so that they can express their thoughts or point of view
- help their teens keep in touch with their old friends

5.5. Making friends

Importance of Friendship

Good friends and friendships are important for teenagers since they give them
- a sense of belonging
- a feeling of being valued
- help with developing confidence
- the sense of security and comfort (since others may have gone through similar experiences)
- information about the changes that puberty brings (physically and emotionally)
- a way to experiment with different values, roles, identities and ideas
- experience in getting along with people of the opposite sex
- a social group to do new things with, things that are different from what families do

Ways of making friends

- To make a new friendship, a teen should
    - Be nice and smile to everyone
    - Talk to other people and make them laugh
    - Help people in the classroom and in the playground
    - Talk to the person who sits next to them
    - As it is easier to get to know one person than to go into a big group
    - Identify some girls or boys in the class with whom they might have more in common and those who could be potential friends
    - Not try to show off; just be themselves
- Parents can help their teenage children make new friends by helping them develop friendship skills by
    - being warm and supportive
    - staying connected and actively listening to them
    - thinking about their interests and strengths
    - supporting them if friendship problems come up
    - praising them when they are fair, trusting and supportive
    - encouraging them to keep working on positive social traits

- o looking for new extracurricular activities
- o encouraging them to engage/participate in social and extra-curricular activities
- o encouraging them to join a club, sports team or social group activity that appeals to them
- o helping them mix with other teens who share similar interests, as it is a great way to start friendships and build confidence
- o helping them plan an activity with friends, such as watching a movie at home, having a sleepover, or playing some sport at the local park
- o taking them and their friends to a movie, the ballet, the circus, a zoo, a museum, a sporting event
- o asking them if they would like to invite a friend over for some structured activity
- o making sure they feels comfortable inviting friends home, and giving them plenty of space when they do so
- o teaching them how to engage in conversation, as small talk is a learned skill and it does not come easily for everyone (it is particularly difficult for teens who are more introverted)
- o helping them understand that having friends, finding new friendships and friendly relationships is an important part of their development

5.6. Friendship Problems – Arguing

- Sometimes teenagers feel unhappy in a friendship, or feel excluded. When conflicts or arguments are present between friends, parents should take action to help them understand that
  - o teen friendships are different than kid friendships
  - o finding friends they can trust, true friends, is not easy and obvious
  - o only a good friendship will make them feel good about themselves
  - o a really good and trustworthy friend can be hard to find
  - o honesty is an important ingredient in a friendship
  - o it takes time to make a good friend and it takes many learned skills to maintain a friendship (it also takes many skills to end a friendship)
  - o being friends does not mean you will never argue
  - o conflicts is a natural part of relationships – even the best of friends are going to have fights, but not every argument means the end of a friendship
  - o friends sometimes hurt each other, but they can always apologize and forgive each other
  - o friends disagreeing can be a sign of a healthy relationship, if it is done respectfully
- To avoid deterioration of their friendship teenagers should
  - o never call their friend names or use physical threats or violence
  - o not broadcast their argument to other people, e.g. by writing about it on social media, or telling other friends about their fight

- stay calm in case of arguing, and if they are getting upset, take time out
- agree to talk to each other again once they have had time to cool off
- try to forgive and move on and not to stay mad for long
- try to move on in the friendship even if they cannot come up with a solution to their argument, agree to disagree
- take a step back and think about whether the argument is worth losing their friendship
- meet somewhere neutral and try to talk calmly about their problem
- express their feelings in a healthy way and not threaten to end the friendship
- try not to make the other person feel guilty
- step back from the persons in argument without removing them from their life entirely. This way can help them stay friendly while respecting each other desire to change things
- end the friendship and make new friends, if there is not any other possibility, and take their focus away from feeling left out

5.7. Obesity

Obesity may become a lifelong issue. Overweight children are much more likely to become overweight adults unless they adopt and maintain healthier patterns of eating and exercise

Causes

The causes of obesity are complex and include genetic, biological, behavioral and cultural factors. Obesity occurs when a person eats more calories than the body burns. General causes of obesity
- poor eating habits
- overeating or binging
- lack of regular exercise
- family history of obesity (If one parent is obese, there is a considerable chance that their child will also be obese. However, when both parents are obese, their children have an even larger chance of being obese)
- medical illnesses (endocrine, neurological problems)
- medications (steroids, some psychiatric medications)
- stressful life events or changes (separations, divorce, moves, deaths, abuse)
- family and peer problems
- low self-esteem
- depression or other emotional problems
- there is a connection between what people know about nutrition and their eating habits
  - people been taught about the need of a varied diet with plenty of vitamins tend to eat more healthily

- o people without this education eat too much junk food and suffer various diseases
- social factors also cause people to eat unhealthily
- many people eat fast food due to lack of time to have a proper meal
- eating habits affect our health
- junk food is a major factor in poor diet and detrimental to health
- eating too much junk food can lead to health issues later in life
- young people eat burgers and pizzas in order to be seen that they are cool and to impress their peers

For any age
- unhealthy eating habits
- relying on cars instead of walking
- less physical demands at work
- preference of inactive leisure activities
- inactive lifestyle which results in burning less calories
- irregularly eating and consumption of large portions of high-calorie food

Consequences/Problems caused

Obesity can affect teen's health in a number of ways. These include:
- high blood pressure and high cholesterol, risk factors for heart disease
- it is the major cause of type 2 diabetes
- it can affect the knees and hips causing joint problems
- it can lead in sleep apnea which cause them breathing problems, stop breathing for brief periods and heavy snoring
- people who are overweight, or obese often suffer psychosocially, because modern culture sees overly thin people as the ideal body size
- teens with weight problems tend to have much lower self-esteem and be less popular with their peers
- depression, anxiety, and obsessive compulsive disorder

For people of any age *obesity may results in*
- physical health problems and loss of productivity
- incorrect functioning of their body that contributes to the risk of developing some chronic illnesses
- As body fat percentage increases, the person's metabolism worsens
- Overweight people are very unhealthy
- Overweight people often suffer from stress and tiredness which lessens their work capacity and results in lower work productivity

Solutions

- Obese children need a thorough medical evaluation to check the possibility of a physical cause and consequently undertake the proper treatment

- To lose weight the number of calories being eaten must be reduced and the level of physical activity to be increased
- Lasting weight loss can only occur when there is a self-motivation
- Making healthy eating and regular exercise a family activity can improve the chances of successful teens' weight control
- Schools should
  - educate students on developing healthy eating habits
  - provide healthy snacks in the cafeteria
  - hand out information on the food pyramid
  - invite a nutritionist to speak
- Obese teenagers should
  - start a weight-management program
  - change eating habits (eat slowly, develop a routine)
  - plan meals and make better food selections (eat less fatty foods, avoid junk and fast foods)
  - control portions and consume less calories
  - increase physical activity (especially walking) and have a more active lifestyle
- Parents should
  - try to influence children and help them lead a healthier lifestyle
  - actively be involved in their children's diet
  - plan eating meals as a family instead of eating while watching television or at the computer
  - cook nutritious meals so that children can eat healthier food and get used to it
  - do not use food as a reward
  - limit snacking
  - sett good examples to pursue
  - talk about nutrition at home
  - attend a diet counselor
- improved health education can help people eat and live better
- It is very hard for governments to make a difference to the choices individual people make
- Governments could
  - ban advertisements for unhealthy foods on television
  - require companies to provide healthy meals for their employees, where applicable

5 8. Following Fashion

Problems

- People follow the latest fashions and buy new clothes every season
- Many people have got into financial difficulty because they are unable to resist buying yet another new outfit

- People spend their hard-earned cash on items that they do not really need

- Appearance has never been more important to people in the Western world than it is today

Young and adult people should
- learn to manage their money properly as it is very important for living well
- calculate what they need in order to be comfortable, avoiding extravagant purchases and trying to put something aside for the future
- shop in sales
- find many items at discount prices
  Refutation:
    o There is often only a limited choice of clothes available
    o Many items are just about to go out of fashion
    o This is the store's way of getting rid of old stock before bringing out the new one
- Visit stores that have top name clothes not sold at normal branches because they are flawed in some way. This way, it is possible to find lovely clothes, such as designer styles, at bargain prices
- This items might have a tiny hole or a slight mark which is either easy to fix or hardly noticeable
  Refutation:
    o They must be careful not to buy something which might prove impossible to repair

5.9. Part time jobs

- Having a job helps a teenager become an adult
- Earning money brings responsibility
- Having to be at work at a certain time and do the job they were hired to do, helps them learn a sense of responsibility, otherwise, they would lose their job
  Refutation:
    o Although learning to be responsible is important, teenagers are also still children
- Working teenager would be able to pay for their own clothes, school supplies, and entertainment
- Working teenager could be saving their money for college or even just to buy something fun that they want for themselves

- Earning and spending their money responsibly helps them mature

- Having a job can
    o interfere with other important aspects of teens' life
    o distract teenager's energy and attention from their schoolwork
    o leave them with little time to relax and be with friends
    o result in sacrificing education for work
- Children have to focus on schoolwork and friends
- Teenage years are the last time children have the chance for a carefree life
- A job could possibly add too much responsibility they are not able to deal with at early age
- Working while studying results in
    o lacking time for education and constantly feeling under pressure
    o lower quality of education and, therefore, has no benefits at all

- Students who work
    o have many financial expenses to meet
    o are lacking of financial resources
    o how to cope with high cost of education (many colleges and universities set high tuition fees)
    o may come from families that cannot fully afford the higher education for their children
    o have to work to pay university and college fees
- Studying away from hometown
    o leads students to have to pay for accommodation, food, entertainment etc
    o forces students to try to earn money to afford their living, as it is often hard for their families to cover these expenses

To reduce the number of working students
- The government could
    o make higher education free
    o finance educational establishments from the State's budget
    o make universities and colleges accessible for everyone
    o promote unpaid e-learning since distance education doesn't require a lot of resources to be maintained and students do not have to leave their homes

5.10. Social Problems

Causes

Social problems involving teenagers have been increased in recent years
* due to modern lifestyles parents spend more and more time at work, are absent from home, have less time to supervise their children and are not in a position to control their children
  Refutation:
  o Working parents are in fact a good example to their children
  o Teenagers who come from hardworking families spend their time on schoolwork and conduct themselves well
  o Teenagers who do create social problems by getting drunk or painting graffiti come from homes where parents are unemployed
* Standards of behavior have fallen among teenagers
* Teenagers leaving school early cannot find work due to lack of qualifications and spend their time on the street with nothing productive to do
* Poor discipline at school along with teachers **inability/failure** of controlling their classes

Solutions

* Parents should bear some responsibility for the actions of their teenage children
* If Parents were at home, then they would be able to make certain that their children did not join gangs and spent their time on socially acceptable activities

5.11. Graffiti

For

* Graffiti may be seen as a way for young people to express their creativity and not an act of vandalism
* For some people it is a form of art, a means for young people, in particular, to express themselves
* There are groups of young people who create wonderful works of art on bare wails using spray paints
* These groups deserve to be praised for their creativity

Against

* For other people it is something destructive, an act carried out by vandals
* Many public buildings, statues and other memorials in towns and cities have been ruined by young people who spray messages all over them

- Graffiti messages are rude and offensive,
- The offenders are invariably teenagers and it would be hard, if not impossible, to defend what they do

- If young people were encouraged to work together to decorate the walls of public buildings, it would give them something worthwhile to do in their free time and brighten up the downtown area

6. Media

6.1. Advertising

Pros/for/advantages/ benefits

- It facilitates consumers' choice as they need assistance to make informed decisions on the a wide array of products on the market
- Consumers do not have the time to find out about the latest developments of specific products and adverts help them
- Companies advertise special offers which is beneficial to the customers
- Advertising helps to keep prices competitive as producers of similar products are forced to lower their prices
- It offers employment opportunities

Cons/against/disadvantages/ negative results/problems

- It leads to overproduction as manufacturers vie for consumer interest resulting in waste of dwindling natural resources
- It causes a huge **litter/waste** problem as it enhances the use of elaborate form of packaging of products in order to make them more appealing to prospective buyers
- It is manipulative, encouraging people to buy products they may not necessarily need
- It may be dangerous as it encourages people, in particular young people, to spend money without thinking, just buying things they do not need
- Advertisement encourages compulsive buying/shopping
- Advertisements encourage people to buy products or services that might be too expensive, unnecessary, or even unhealthy
- Children and young people are most influenced by advertisements
- Advertisement aimed at children are more manipulative, as children cannot critically judge what products they really need
- Many times children put enormous pressure on their parents to buy specific products
- The way many advertisements encourage people to buy products they may not need or cannot afford is often unethical
- The market has the tendency to idealize life
- Many advertisements try to create insecurities within consumers

- Frequently, advertisements attempt to sell a lifestyle rather than only the product itself, because this lifestyle may result in even more consumption
- Many advertisement spots or campaigns convey the message that without the advertized products, people are inferior to their peers
- Many advertisements make outrageous claims about the products they promote and are misleading
- Most advertisements are annoying, intrusive and irritating, as they are everywhere, and there are only very few places we can avoid them

Reasons

- There are nowadays so many different ways companies promote their products and services, ranging from television commercials to simple flyers, we cannot protect ourselves from being exposed to the influential power of advertisements
- We cannot avoid advertising due to the enormous number of products produced by different producers
- There are very few places we can actually avoid adverts. They are almost in any place:
  - on television
  - on the world wide web
  - in the street
  - on our mobile phones via SMS
  - in football matches
  - in blockbuster movie

Solutions

- Some restrictions could be placed concerning the kind of products advertised (smoking: cigarette adverts have been banned in many countries) and the method used
- Consumers should use their commonsense when they go to the shops, and buy only what they really need
- Parents should
  - protect their children from excessive exposure to advertising
  - explain them the real aim of advertisements
  - encourage them not to pay too much attention to the advertisements
  - in extreme cases, if possible, turn the television off

Problems/Negative Results/Consequences

- Celebrities are often forced to endure constant harassment, being followed stealthily by paparazzi
- Many newspapers, especially tabloids, do not hesitate to distort the truth in order to gain increased circulation
- Some newspapers or TV shows exploit the pain of ordinary people and publish tragedy stories sensationalizing them, with no regard for the victims' pain and suffering
- What will be published on the media (be broadcasted on TV/radio, or printed in newspapers) id determined only by the journalists, taking into consideration only the profit
- The point of view many newspaper take on a particular issue may be biased
- Concerning Political issues, newspapers take usually a more supportive position of the government site, or an opposite one without caring really about the real truth

Causes/Reasons

- Media play a central role in contemporary society, keeping us abreast of current events and issues
- Media sometimes cannot resist the temptation to exploit their role and manipulate the public
- Media cannot survive for long if they do not attract customers to buy the papers they publish, or view or listen to the stories they broadcast
- Some newspaper editors or broadcasters have cannot disconnect heir political leanings from their job and affect the tone of the stories they print or broadcast

Solutions

- Governments should protected people's private lives by setting strict limits on the media intrusion into their personal lives
- The media should not abuse situations harming people's personal dignity
- Each article or reportage should be checked by an internal board whether it could be published while preserving the privacy and dignity of the individuals but not exploiting them
- However, excessive external control could result in censorship, a dangerous situation that accumulates too much power in the hands of governments who can determine what the media can or cannot say

7. Animal Rights

7.1. Animal Testing

Pros/ for/ advantages/benefits

- Medical research involving animals has dramatically improved the health of the human race
- Animal experiments may help us find cures for difficult diseases like cancer
- Humanity would be at the mercy of any deadly infection, would we rely only on alternative methods of medicaments testing and research
- They facilitate research in genetic engineering
- They are necessary before any drug can be piloted on a small group of patients
- Without animal testing many procedures or new drugs would be extremely unsafe for human use
- Animal testing is so far the most effective experimentation method available
- There is no viable alternative; realistic tests are necessary
- There are no alternative methods instead of animal experimentation, except in some cases as experiments in-vitro
- Testing on humans (children or adults) is even more inhumane, both morally and ethically wrong and therefore not acceptable
- It is better to suffer animals than humans
- Direct use of new drugs in humans could have disastrous results that cannot be foreseen. Many people would die until a healthy result is obtained
- Alternative methods of testing, such as computer models or testing on plants, are by no means advanced enough
- Many famous lifesaving drugs have been invented this way
- Animals used for experiments (laboratory animals) are bred for this specific purpose and do not result in reduction of the number of wild animals on the planet
- Despite the fact that humans and animals are different genetically, there are considerable similarities and animal testing provides important information that could not be achieved in human testing

Cons/against/disadvantages

- Animals feel as much pain as humans do
- Animal experiments are unkind and cause animals a lot of pain, therefore, they should be treated respectfully

- Animals suffer when they are kept in cages for long periods
- Secret filming in laboratories have shown cruelty to animals
- Not all animal tests are really important
- Animals are not only used to test new medicines but also new cosmetics, which could be tested on humans instead
- A lot of experiments are conducted for reasons of little importance such as the testing of cosmetics, and not to find cures for diseases, so they are unnecessary
- Although some animals undergo similar physical processes to humans, it is a fact that humans and animals are different genetically
- It is useless to use animals in experiments to see the effects of some substances on humans since they are different genetically
- It is better to use humans directly, as the results of experiments on animals cannot be as valid and reliable as the same been done on humans
- Sometimes experiments on animals give wrong results because animals' bodies are not exactly the same as our own
- Many experiments are ineffective, as they are not applicable to humans
- Numerous products whereas have been considered effective on animals, they are, in fact, unsafe for human use. **Example**: a large number of commercial drugs have been withdrawn from the market because of side-effects on humans
- Many times computer simulation is possible

- Control of unnecessary testing should be applied
- Advanced computer modeling could make the use of many laboratory animals unnecessary

7.2. Animal Captivity - Zoos

- Zoos protect endangered species as natural habitats are being destroyed by human activities such as farming, logging, and creation of urban settlements
- Humans have destroyed the habitats of many animal species, putting their survival at risk
- Zoos protect orphaned young animals ended up in them or in wildlife parks (after their parents have been killed in the wild for sport or for their fur) in order to ensure their survival
- Many zoos actually help to protect endangered species
- Special breeding programs carried out in many zoos are actually saving some species from extinction
- Zoos have breeding programs to replenish the number of threatened species by releasing the bred animals back into the wild
- Zoos allow scientific study of animals and their behavior

- Zoos can play an educational role as people can see animals they may never be able to see otherwise
- Visiting the zoo is a pleasurable experience for many humans
- Zoos and circus provide for the people the opportunity to see exotic animals that normally they would never have a chance to see up close in their natural habitats
- Animals being bred in captivity have never known their natural habitat and hence do not suffer
- There are zoos that have made the captivity conditions as comfortable as possible for all animals they have
- Zoos are fully aware of the fact that if the public feels that the animals are not being properly cared for, they will not bring their children to the zoo
- Keeping domestic animals, such as dogs and cats, in apartments with no plenty of space do not cause any suffer since these animal have been specifically bred for providing company and comfort and are, by and large, kept well by their owners
- Keeping exotic animals in home provides the opportunity to expose children, as well as adults, to a highly entertaining and educational experience

Cons/ against/opponents

- Zoos and circuses only exist as a form of entertainment
- Circuses only train wild animals to perform tricks
- In circuses, when the animals are no longer capable of performing to the expected standards they are put down or even starved to death
- In some zoos and circuses the animals are maltreated, the living conditions are poor
- Many zoos and circuses do not have the financial resources required to maintain the animals living conditions in an appropriate level
- In some zoos the animals are fed scraps of food instead of hunting or foraging
- In some zoos and circuses the animal are raised by cruel trainers instead of their real mothers
- Animals kept in cramped cages in zoos are deprived of their basic needs
- Captivity is not a natural state for wild animals
- In captivity the wild animals are not given the opportunity to live free, instead they are forced to spend their lives performing ridiculous tricks to entertain the audience
- Imprisoning animals in circuses is unethical and utterly atrocious
- In zoos and circuses animals are viewed as nothing more than commodities to be bought, used and discarded
- Keeping wild animals in captivity has always been a controversial subject
- Keeping any animal locked up in an unnatural environment is a form of cruelty
- Animals frequently miss the company of their family group so much that they suffer from depression and get sick
- Not all zoos are the same

- There are zoos whose conditions are poor and the animals are kept in dirty, cramped spaces
- In inappropriately maintained zoos, the animals are unable to run around freely and have very little to do all day **except for/apart from** sleep
- Many domestic animals keepers have no interest in their animal well-being
- Often, domestic animals are beaten if they misbehave, and deprived of basic veterinarian care

7.3. Animal/Wildlife Protection

Problems

- Many human activities often cause massive extinctions of various species, deplete local flora and fauna, threatening the biodiversity/ cause loss of biodiversity
- Human activities often deplete local flora and fauna and cause loss of bio-diversity
- Many human activities can change the natural environment having negative impacts on the world's ecosystem
- Many human activities transform the environment and destroy the vegetation and animals' natural habitat
- By building new roads people are cutting down the trees, cementing the soil, and altering the environment
- The environment in many areas of the planet is already under threat, and urgent action is needed to protect it
- Change of habitats and overexploitation of natural resources cause species extinction
- Many species of indigenous plants, birds, and insects are threatened because their habitats is being destroyed and used as farmland
- Intensive activities of harvesting of natural resources may exhaust them
- Too frequent/intensive fishing does not leave enough time for fish to reproduce. As a consequence fish population cannot recover leading to disappearing of the more vulnerable species
- Too frequent fishing does not leave enough time for fish to reproduce and makes them disappear

Solution

- On way of ensuring that natural habitats and creatures that live in them are protected is to set up conservation areas where human activity and development are limited
- We must protect the natural habitats to ensure that the creatures living in them can survive

- Natural areas can be protected by setting up conservation areas where human activity is limited
- In protected areas the human activity is limited and as a consequence the overexploitation of their resources is avoided
- Untouched environment must be saved and the endangered species be prevented from dying out
- The awareness among people should be promoted by informing the general population about the dangers of bio-diversity loss
- People consciousness of the environment should be enhanced so that not overuse or destroy the natural resources
- The extinction of endangered species could be lessen significantly by protecting natural areas and enlightening people to this problem

- Animals are part of the live on Earth and should get help in order to survive from human activities
- Humans have destroyed the natural habitats of some wild animals by the accelerated pace of civilization
- The expansion of civilization leads to the distortion of the food chain for many species, and thus discords the balance of the ecosystem
- Many species of indigenous plants, birds, and insects in the area are threatened because their habitats is being destroyed and used as farmland
- Endangered species could be saved and natural ecosystems preserved
- In the long run, humans will suffer from the abuse of animals and ecosystems
- Establishing of conservation areas, in order to protect endangered species and preserve the countryside, benefits not only the wildlife but the local population as well
- In conservation areas endangered species can be saved and natural ecosystems preserved, as they are protected by law
- Restricting farming and industry in some areas reduces the amount of polluting chemicals released into **the ground water/rivers/lakes/sea**
- As ground water is used by many communities to water supply, protecting aquatic habitats from polluting anthropogenic activities should be in the interests of local people too
- Making an area a conservation area we ensure its survival for future generation
- Preserved areas of unspoiled natural beauty could be used for recreational activities
- Conservation areas stimulate local economy by attracting visitors from other areas
- Local businesses benefit from the application of the green tourism principle

- Large quantities of resources have been used to protect animals in the wilderness while
  - Humans are still suffering in the war-torn countries or disaster-stricken areas
  - Many countries suffer from extreme climatic conditions making impossible an adequate harvest and a large number of people face the shortage of food, shelter and clothing
  - In many countries people cannot feed themselves better than the wild animals, despite the international aid

8. Legal Issues

Reasons

- The demoralization of social conditions has contributed on the increase in the crime rate
- The imbalanced way children are grown up/nurtured by their parents
- Many children are neglected by their parents as many of them have to work and therefore are not around to give their children support when needed
- Under certain conditions, poverty may induce crime as poor people, including children in poor families, may resort to illegal means, steal or rob, when become desperate, in order to survive or to sustain their families
- However, poverty is not an inevitable cause of crime and
  - The opinion that a person is more likely to be a criminal just because they are poor it is preposterous
  - Poverty and crime have different sources:
    - ✓ poverty is the result of economic inferiority
    - ✓ crime is the result of demoralization
  - Both the rich and the poor could be involved in crime

- Juvenile delinquency differs from adult criminality: young offenders
  - Are mentally immature
  - May be unaware of the consequences of what they are about to do, or even what they have done
  - May commit a crime unwittingly or on impulse

Solutions

- Imposing harsher/stricter punishment for the crime committed
- Severe punishments act as a deterrent to would-be criminals, while too often, the courts are too lenient
- Reconsider punishment for certain crimes
- Stricter prison sentences and fines deter prospective criminals from resorting to illegal acts
- However, long prison sentences should be limited only for those who commit serious crimes (assault or murder)

- Establishing better re-education and rehabilitation systems for reforming offenders/criminals
- Community service could give an offender the opportunity to offer something positive to society, improving their character
- Imprisoning: Isolate dangerous individuals from the rest of society
- Improving education and social services for all so that gradually to disappear the need to commit a crime in order to survive
- Increase the numbers of police officers and police patrols in local communities and in areas with high criminality to deter criminal activity and increase the safety feeling
- Potential criminals are discouraged by frequent police presence and commit fewer crimes
- Installing Closed Circuit Television Cameras (CCTV) in public places acts as a crime deterrent
- Media should present more stories in the news about how crime is being tackled rather than focus on the negative aspect of any criminal act
- Radical improvements should be made to ensure a better standard of living
- Government's resources should focus on tackling the causes of crime, preventing it and leading to less crime in the future
- Governments should attempt to tackle poverty through better income distribution
- More job opportunities should be provided for the poor and the unemployed, as crime rates are the highest among these groups of people
- Juvenile delinquents should not be punished by the legal system in the same way as adult criminals
- Parents have to take more responsibility for their children's actions
- Parents could also be punished if their children commit a crime
- Harsh punishment decisions may ruin the life of young offenders
- Juvenile offenders should be treated according to their age
- Older juvenile offenders should be punished with greater severity than younger because they are more aware of the implications of what they have done
- Young criminals' imprisonment with older, more hardened criminals may have harmful influences
- Juvenile reform schools, if well organized and well managed, are more suitable and more effective places for correcting young people's behavior than prisons

- Provides an opportunity for rehabilitation and re-education for the convicted
- Acts as a deterrent
- Criminals are not only punished, but also remove them from society so that to be reassured that they will not commit more crimes for the duration of the imprisonment
- Allows to scale punishments effectively and as a result, the disincentive to commit crimes increases with the increasing severity of the crime

Cons/against/disadvantages

- Prison process is not working, at least it is not completely effective
- The prison environment is often conducive to criminalization rather than rehabilitation
- Prisoners convicted for minor offences mix with criminals have committed severe crimes and so their character will not improve
- Young people enter prison for minor offences and come out equipped with the skills to commit more serious crimes
- Prisons are very expensive
- Overcrowded prisons become difficult to manage

8.3. Longer Prison Sentences to Reduce Crime

For

- Spending someone who has committed a serious offence, such as assault, a long time in prison provides them an opportunity to get rehabilitated
- It acts as a deterrent for someone who is thinking of committing a crime

Against

- Leaving people in prison for a long time means that they will mix with other criminals and so their character will not improve at all
- Community service is a most effective alternative
- Community service gives an offender the opportunity to give something positive back to society, and it may improve their character
- Long prison sentences should remain for those who commit serious crimes such as assault or murder

8.4. Capital punishment

Pros/for/advantages/ benefits

- It is deemed as an effective deterrent of major crimes as it may prevent a person from committing crime by show the adverse consequences of such actions
- The best method to prevent a person from committing crime is to show the consequences of their actions
- By killing criminals, the danger to society is being reduced
- The governments spend large sums of national budget on maintenance of prisoners
- This money can be used for the development of the society and welfare of the people

Cons/against/disadvantages

- None has the rights to kill other humans, as the right to live is a basic right of any human being, and no one can infringe it
- It is a flawed idea that by killing criminals the danger to society is reduced because it fails to realize the fact that criminals that have committed serious crimes inevitably get life sentences and are never released back into society, thus ensuring the general public's safety
- Killing criminals makes things worse than better due to the fact that neither their crimes can be corrected, nor can they compensate the humanity for their crimes
- In case of murder, killing the guilty person cannot bring the dead person in live again, and so execution helps nobody else apart from the relatives who might want the criminal to die out of a sense of revenge
- Innocent people can face wrongful execution
- Possible unfair sentences take away lives of innocent people and make other citizens lose faith in law and justice
- Capital punishment do not give criminals a second chance to repent of their acts in order to improve themselves

8.5. School Violence

Reasons

- Schools discipline is not always strict enough so there is considerable room for difficult students to deviate from the acceptable behavior
- Puberty, as it is a critical period characterized by oversensitivity and even instability provokes many adolescents into reacting emotionally
- Teenagers who suffer from depression, experience increased pressure concerning their personal lives, or have an inferiority complex often vent their feelings on others, or go on a rampage and destroy school property
- The influence of the peers plays an important role
- Teenagers are highly influenced by their classmates and tend to imitate each other's behavior without using critical judgment
- Acts of vandalism are usually committed by groups rather than individuals

Solutions

- The educational system must be changed aiming to prevent and correct students disruptive behavior
- Stricter measures should be implemented so that they can act as a deterrent for social disruptions
- The installation of surveillance cameras may deter some delinquent acts, as well as guards that patrol the school yard
- Teacher can also patrol the school yard, oversee the school hall and recreational areas
- Teacher should keep an eye to students to check whether they engage in any disorderly behavior
- Professional counseling and psychological support should be provided instead of harsh punitive measures to help students cope with their difficulties
- Schools should promote collaboration and respect among peers

Reasons

- Athletes are desperate to win and some of them seem to be willing to do anything to increase their chances of winning

Consequences

- Doping enables athletes to influence the outcomes in their favor, and defeat their opponents who have trained and worked hard
- Doping does irreparable damage to the users leading to hormone imbalance, organ failure and in extreme cases death
- Enhanced athletes' performance due doping can be described as unnatural
- The use of chemical substances to enhance sports' performance is unethical, against the principle of good sportsmanship, and therefore it can be considered a crime

Solutions

- Only **severe repercussions/ harsh punishment** will act as a deterrent discouraging players and coaches from resorting to such harmful substances to attain victory
- Athletes been caught have done use of illegal and forbidden substances should been disqualified and deprived of their past medals

9. Environment

9.1. Environment Protection

Reasons

- The environment is in danger
- Mankind has caused the world's environmental problems

Solution/Actions

- For most environmental problems only governments and businesses can take action to solve them, e.g. pollution from factories and cars. Nevertheless, there are also things that individuals can do
- Governments must force factories to reduce their pollution, and car manufacturers to produce cars which emit less exhaust fumes
- Individuals can recycle their used plastic, glass and paper
- By recycling, factories will not have to produce so much packaging products, leading to less pollution
- Individuals can use their cars as little as possible, reducing pollution
- We should stop using our cars so much and start cycling or walking a little more
- Instead of commuting by car, we could possibly do it on foot or by bike
- We ought to start reduce the quantity of rubbish we produce, not throw away so many things, instead reuse them, and recycle most of our waste
- Individuals can raise awareness about environmental issues, and put pressure on governments and businesses to act responsibly
- We should teach young pupils about the dangers of contamination and pollution
- Educating the young people is the only way to change the future, because they are the future citizens of the world

9.2. Global Warming

Causes/Reasons

- Global warming is the result of the way contemporary humans live their lives
- Industrial emissions of greenhouse gases (such as carbon-dioxide, methane) in earth's atmosphere are enormous
- Greenhouse gases trap and absorb atmospheric heat back to earth surface

- Trapped thermal energy in the atmosphere ultimately causes an increase on earth's surface temperature leading consequently to global warming and greenhouse effect
- Burning fossil fuels in power plants for electricity production and in transport means for transportation leads to carbon dioxide emissions
- Fossil fuels use for transportation continues to increase because of our resort in private cars' use, increasing worldwide goods consumption and therefore increasing need to transport goods

Effects/Impact

- The latest scientific prediction about the global temperature levels are worrying
- As the world's is becoming warmer and warmer the weather conditions change
- Changing weather leads to regional climate changes affecting the local and regional ecosystems
- Climate changes may cause higher or lower agricultural yields, further glacial retreat, reduced summer stream flows, and endangered species extinctions
- Rising sea level may cause coastal cities and ports to be submerged under sea-water and many islands to vanish
- The water balance disturbances, its changing spatial and temporal distribution will bring water lack in some parts of the world while other regions might become wetter than they are now
- Water availability crisis may be the most serious and perhaps the most expensive to deal with
- The amount and the pattern of precipitation will change dramatically making relevant predictions hard to made and the uncertainty regarding regional rain forecasts may grow
- The frequency, duration, and intensity of extreme weather events, such as floods, droughts, heat waves, and tornadoes may increase as a result of the changes in surface temperature and the precipitation pattern
- New pattern of agricultural cultivations may emerge whose effects on the ecosystems are fairly unpredictable
- The human health will be put at risk as the spread of major tropical diseases will change unpredictably
- As the earth becomes warmer (higher earth's temperatures and changing climate), more and more people are likely to be affected by tropical diseases like malaria

Solution

- The rate of the global warming process has to slow down by reducing the amount of carbon dioxide and the other greenhouse gases we produce
- Less fossil fuels has to be used and resorting into eco-friendly energy sources is the only answer
- The dependence on fossil fuel use must be reduced and alternative forms of energy must be promoted

- Alternative and environmentally friendly energy sources are wind and solar power
- Renewable energy sources must be made accessible to all citizens
- Greener alternative forms of energy must be developed by scientist and engineers and funded and promoted by governments
- Thermal power generating stations must be reduced, reducing at the same time our dependence on fossil fuels (and consequently the quantity if carbon dioxide we emit into the environment, a major greenhouse gas) for generating electricity
- Reforestation is far more effective if carried out to a wider extent
- Public efforts should be made in order for the cities and neighborhoods to become greener
- Education is a better, more effective, long-term and a lasting solution
- Education is the key to achieve any environmental goal
- All people need to learn to live in a way greener and kinder to the environment
- People of all ages could be educated about the environmental consequences of their actions by programs supported by the governments
- People should buy cars with the best fuel economy
- Cars should be used only when really necessary
- Factories could be obliged by law to use environmentally friendly energy sources
- Governments should make recycling, composting, and the reforestation of areas which are lacking in vegetation compulsory
- People should/could
  - Recycle, compost and purchase environmentally friendly products
  - Try to conserve electricity by not using it wastefully
  - Reduce heating and air conditioning use
  - Opt for public transport or bicycles instead of private vehicles
  - Use energy efficient light bulbs

9.3. Waste disposal

Waste management ways

- Incineration
- Landfill
- Recycling
- Energy recovery by converting rubbish

Problems

- Improper **waste/garbage** disposal **result in/is associated with** innumerable and mostly irreversible problems
- Waste incineration, though has been proposed as a way of trash disposal may lead into even worse air pollution problems

- Incineration installations that do not work properly **emit/produce** fumes and toxic gases which result in atmospheric pollution and health damage, e.g. respiratory problems
- Incineration (garbage burning) may cause atmospheric pollution and consequently respiratory problems in case the installation does not work properly
- Dumping litter into landfills is far from an adequate way of dealing with the problem
- Landfill operations have the potential to considerably cause great damage to the environment
- Toxic substances from deposited trash in landfill dumping may seep into the ground water below the landfill sites, contaminating it
- Rainwater washes through the half-buried garbage toxic substances seeping them into the ground water underneath the landfill contaminating it
- Contaminated water may be used to irrigate crops, as drinking water, end up in river systems and eventually into the sea affecting marine life

Reasons

- Many urban areas are facing an alarming waste management crisis as their landfills are or will be nearly running out in the coming years (landfills have started to run out)
- The increasing earth population (population growth) generates bigger volume of wastes than in the past
- Improved life conditions coupled with technology development leads to production of various types of waste
- The unprecedented economic development has led to production of various classes of waste
- The industrial growth and the sprawl of urban areas have led to a significant increase in hazardous and non- hazardous waste generation
- Waste is putting on the environment without any treatment
- Trash is typically buried in landfills or incinerated, resulting in air and water pollution

Solutions

- Authorities should focus on controlling the waste production and improve the waste management
- Authorities should use the advancement in science and technology to manage waste production and treatment
- Technologies that handle waste in environment-friendly and cost-efficient manner should be adopted
- Gasification processes that can turn wastes into energy may lessen our dependence on fossil fuels and eventually totally eliminate the use of landfills
- Recycling items made from glass, aluminum, or plastic is one of the best ways to eliminate refuse of the raw materials that can be used again

- Recycling must be done on a large scale in order to be effective
- Recycling is only feasible if local authorities provide collection points for recyclable material in convenient locations
- Individuals/Consumers can help reduce waste by
    - changing their habits and trying to make full use of things, or make other uses of them, that otherwise would be thrown away
    - passing on unwanted items, such as electrical goods or cloths, to others, rather than disposing of them
    - altering their consumer habits so that they produce less waste (trash)
    - preferring products that do not use excessive amounts of unnecessary packaging, as most of the times they aims at only making the product attractive
    - reusing bags than throw them away, or preferably to switch to long-lasting cotton bags, reducing the widespread use of plastic shopping bags (plastic is not biodegradable)
- Manufactures that use packaging that does not conform to environmentally friendly standards should be strictly fined
- Educating people in order to enhance their awareness at all levels of waste production and management, especially what concerns waste recycling, is by far the most effective way of dealing with the problem

9.4. Nuclear Technology

Pros/ for/ advantages/ benefits

- The threat of using nuclear weapons maintains world peace
- Nuclear power provides cheap and clean energy
- Nuclear power is the most inexpensive source of electricity
- Nuclear energy is virtually limitless and therefore can solve the problem of the increasing energy demands
- Nuclear power plants are far cleaner than conventional fuel power plants as they do not combust fossil fuels
- Nuclear power plants are the greener alternative to fossil fuels burning since they do not have negative effects such as global warming and greenhouse effect and atmospheric pollution

Cons/against/disadvantages

- The risk of nuclear warfare and nuclear disasters is great as many adverse incidences have shown
- In nuclear accident, radioactive substances are released into the atmosphere and the water, contaminating at least the local environment with dire consequences

- The production of radioactive waste, such as plutonium, and the problem of its disposal remains unsolved as plutonium remains radioactive for thousands of years

9.5. Overpopulation

Causes

- The decline in the death rate and the increase in the overall birth rate and has resulted in a significant growth of the world's population
- The technological advancement has affected the balance between birth and death rates which has been permanently disturbed
- Technological advancement and discoveries in medical science improved the fertility treatment methods rendering it possible for couples who are unable to conceive to have their own babies
- Due to modern techniques and improved treatment methods pregnancy is today far safer, leading into a rise in birth rate
- Many medical science discoveries have provided better medical facilities and humanity is now able to defeat a whole range of diseases
- Illnesses that had claimed thousands of lives in the past are now cured owning to the invention of vaccines
- The increase in food supply combined with the lower mortality rate have affected the population balance and tipped it in favor of the overpopulation
- Science and technology have produced better means of producing food which allowed more people to feed
- Most developing nations have large number of people who are illiterate, live below the poverty line and have little or no knowledge about family planning.

Effects/Problems

- Overpopulation is causing problems not only for the poor, underdeveloped countries, but also for industrialized developed countries
- Overpopulation, the growing number of people on the planet, can lead to the overexploitation and depletion of the natural resources
- Earth can only provide with goods, such as water and food, only a limited amount of people
- The overuse of resources, such as coal, oil and natural gas leads to irreversible degradation of the environment, and to adverse environmental problems
- The rise in the number of vehicles and industries can badly affected the air quality and **scale up/increase** the consequences of global warming
- Overpopulation especially in developing countries puts a major strain on the available resources resulting in starvation

- In developing countries there are difficulties in providing enough food to feed the increasing population
- Despite the increased food production, owning to the development of science and technology in agriculture and animal breeding, the demand on food supply of the population of the world cannot be satisfied
- Natural disasters and famines bring people in overpopulated areas on the edge of starvation
- Shortage of available resources leads to conflicts over resources' domination becoming a permanent source of tension between neighboring countries which can result in wars
- Unemployment rises in overpopulated countries as there are fewer jobs available to support the large number of people
- Unemployment and overcrowding may lead to crime rise as people, in particular young people, resort to desperate actions, as stealing, to feed their families and to provide them basic amenities of life, or they turn to crime or drugs
- The difference between demand and supply, due to overpopulation, raises the prices of various commodities including food, shelter and healthcare
- Many people have to pay more to survive and feed their families, especially the poor
- Overpopulation exerts great pressure on infrastructures leading to overcrowding and poor quality living in many large cities
- More people, large population, means more demand for education, medical care, transport, housing, and energy consumption
- Poor living conditions cause significant health problems, resulting in illness, such as bronchitis or pneumonia

Solutions

- Awareness and education about overpopulation, enacting birth control measures and regulations, and providing universal access to birth control devices and family planning, could be implemented as mitigation measures in order to reduce the rising course, and its adverse impacts, of overpopulation
- To reduce or to eliminate the crime due to the overpopulation, effective policing of inner city areas would be beneficial
- To combat the increased rate of Earth resources consumption, governments should encourage research on alternative and renewable sources
- To satisfy the rising energy demand, governments should implement appropriate measures to replace the traditional energy sources with renewable sources
- Countries with a food surplus could donate what they do not need to the less fortunate countries to alleviate their population who suffer from starvation
- Combating poverty in developing and overcrowded countries needs international co-operation
- Although it can be considered immoral to enforce family planning so that the world population to can be controlled, governments facing severe overpopulation

problems must educate their citizens about the dangers of a large population and
provide incentives to those who limit the size of their families

9.6. Living in a City and Traffic Problems

Problems/Consequences

- Workers and students are of the most populous groups of victims due to the
  traffic, they are late to work, appointments, classes, and need extra waiting time
- The proliferation of private cars on the roads in many parts of the world has led to
  serious problems of air pollution
- Pollution caused by cars is a serious problem in the modern world

Reasons

- Society has become more mobile than even before and more people need to
  commute to work by car than in the past
- Cars are more affordable for the average consumer than ever before, they are no
  longer a luxury item
- Most families own more than one car
- Cars have become a status symbol
- Improved road networks make it easier to travel
- People do not share car journeys
- Public transport systems for the urban dwellers is in many cities often unreliable,
  inadequate, inconvenient and sometimes unavailable
- Public transport in many cities is very poor, insufficient and ineffective
- Many times there are only old buses and trains that people would rather not use
- In many cities, bus and train services have been reduced because of the difficulty
  in funding them
- It is not seldom bus and train services schedules to be unreliable, resulting in late
  bus arrivals, or arrival in bunches
- Many people live in suburban areas and work in the city

Solutions

- Incentives should be provided to drivers to share journeys
- Advertising campaigns to highlight the negative consequences of using private
  cars in the city
- Governments should discourage people from driving to work by car by
  introducing special tariffs for using the roads, especially during peak periods
- Taxing private cars very heavily and use the money to provide free or cheaper rail
  and bus travel would be a possible solution
- Local authorities should improve the reliability of public transport systems

- Adding more bus or train routes could encourage people to take the bus or the train rather than get in the car
- There should be more pedestrian areas in towns, as well as specific areas where cars entering is prohibited
- Governments should spend money for the development of better public transportation systems and improve their reliability in order to help alleviate this problem
- It is better to spend money for the development of electric and other specific types of cars that may cause less pollution
- Any technology that is developed to improve cars can also improve public transportation
- The city's transportation network could be upgraded by introducing bicycle lanes
- Buses can run on electricity or hydrogen as well as cars can

- Is an ecological solutions to traffic congestion
- Is a realistic alternative to the polluting vehicles
- It is inexpensive to install and maintain lanes
- Encourages healthy exercise and promote physical fitness

- Cyclists can easily have accidents and inhale toxic exhaust fumes
- They are inconvenient for long commuter journey
- Car drivers use bicycle lanes to overtake or park their vehicles

- Discourage car owners from using their cars because it would become very expensive
- Encourage people to use public transport as it would be cheaper
- People would begin to make use of public transport reducing the number of cars on the road and hence cut down on traffic jams (traffic problems) and air pollution as well
- High taxes would generate enough money to make the necessary changes and develop infrastructure
- Save fossil fuels/ natural resources
- Good public transport would increase the mobility of the people

- High taxes would be a heavy burden on the car drivers
- Taxes are already high for a lot of people, and further taxes would only affect poor people or those who may have no choice but to drive every day
- There is not any other door-to-door service like cars
- People like owning and using their cars
- Increased taxes are always unpopular
- Cheap public transport is feasible only by state subsidies
- It takes time to develop the infrastructure for effective public transport

Car Advantages

- More than two people can travel together. A car can take more passengers
- Gives quality time with co-passengers making journeys more pleasant
- Fast access to shopping malls, work etc.
- Greater mobility to old and invalid people
- Owning a car is convenient as you can go anywhere you want whenever you want
- You are not limited to the places the bus and subway routes take you
- You do not have to rely on bus or subway schedules
- Everyone enjoys the freedom a car gives

Car Disadvantages

- Parking problems (lack of space and parking fees). Finding a secure place to park your car in heavily built residential areas is difficult. It requires a lot of patience and luck
- Pollution (toxic emissions from exhaust pipes)
- High costs (insurance, tax, repairs, petrol, etc.)

Motorbike Advantages

- It is more flexible in heavy traffic
- More flexible in traffic
- You can move forward through the gaps leaving the endless lines of cars behind you
- Easier to park
- Lower running costs

Motorbike Disadvantages

- There is a high number of motorcycle accidents
- Exposure to all weather conditions
- Easy to steal

Causes

- **Careless driving/reckless behavior** on the part of drivers
- Breaking the speed limit contributes to thousands of crashes
- Excessive speeding
- Young drivers in particular can't resist the temptation of driving too fast.
- Driving under the influence of alcohol
- People who drink and drive are far more likely to cause crashes than those who abstain
- Even a little alcohol makes people less alert
- Being distracted while driving by using mobile phones
- Bad road condition
- Tiredness. Drivers try unsuccessfully to fight off sleepiness by opening a window or turning up the radio

Solutions

- Governments/authorities should
  - Improve roads' condition ensuring that the road network is safe for drivers (Improved and safer roads provide better driving conditions resulting in fewer accidents)
  - Repair the road on a regular basis taking into consideration factors such as difficult weather conditions and the general deterioration of roads
  - Raise the difficulty level of driving test (Only well qualified drivers would be given a license)
  - Introduce stricter legislation to prevent dangerous practices and impose severe penalties on those who break the law (driving safety conditions)
  - Introduce heavier penalties on drivers who violate traffic regulations in the hope that this will improve safety on our roads, which are becoming more crowded day by day
  - Impose more severe penalties for dangerous driving (e.g. drunk driving, speed violations)
  - Implement intensive police surveillance of traffic laws (e.g. speed limit, wearing helmets/seatbelts) (Fatalities during accidents would be significantly reduced)
  - Install surveillance cameras that can act as deterrent discouraging drivers from speeding (Drivers would be deterred from breaking laws due to heavy fines)
  - Intensify the traffic education to raise public awareness of the causes of car accidents and their repercussions (car accidents, fatalities, injured people) preventing deterioration of the problem
- Traffic education could be achieved via Educational campaigns launched through the media or in schools, or the invitation of traffic police to schools to give talks on the importance of road safety even on behalf of the pedestrians

- **Individuals/drivers/pedestrians** should
  - Always wear seatbelts and ensure that all passengers are doing so as well
  - Adhere to the traffic code (to not drink when they are to drive, not exceed the speed limit and not use their cell phones when are behind the wheel)
  - Pedestrians ought to adhere to the traffic code too
  - Be considerate of other drivers on the road and not drive aggressively or perform other tasks which could distract them, such as eating or smoking
- Frequent and widespread use of alcohol tests by traffic police
- If drivers are aware they will be stopped for this, they will refrain from drinking
- Drivers likely to be overcome by tiredness should be targeted in their cars (This can be accomplished with radio spots and advertising in highway service areas)
- Much heavier penalties must be introduced for speeding (If road users know they will lose their license or face a lengthy prison sentence, they will think twice before accelerating)

9.8. Accidents Involving Young Drivers

Causes

- Passing the driving test and getting a license opens up a whole new world of independence to young people
- increasing number of accidents involve young, inexperienced drivers
- The legal age for obtaining a driving license should be higher than it is now.
- Teenagers are not mature enough to take on the responsibilities that go with driving a car on the public highway
- They see the fact that they have their license as an opportunity for greater freedom, to have fun with their friends or to raise their status in the eyes of their peers

Solutions

- Raising the legal age for obtaining a driver's license

9.9. Globalization

Pros/for/advantages/ benefits

- Decreases manufacturing costs as multinational companies can establish their factories in countries with low labor costs
- Lower manufacturing costs increase profits for companies but also decreases the costs to the consumer

- Lower manufacturing costs decreases the price of the products due to increased manufacturing volume and competition resulting in an increased standard of living of the consumer
- Lower manufacturing costs increase profits for companies but also decreases the costs to the consumer
- The competition between companies in different countries drives prices down benefiting the consumer
- Free global trade improves the global economy and promotes global economic growth
- Companies across the world are able to trade with another with reduced restrictions on importing and exporting goods
- The companies can reach a huge and rapidly expanding market that improves the living conditions all over the world
- Globalization provides poor countries with the chance to develop economically through influx of foreign capital and technology
- Workers from all over the world can move freely from country to country with relative ease and market their skills and services to a worldwide range, in areas where need of people with their skills exists
- Skilled workers can now work overseas and earn more money getting higher wages
- Countries that suffer from gaps in their labor can import them from another country
- Different countries are joining together making common political and economical decisions instead of only focusing on local areas, that benefits the people all over the world
- People from all over the world can communicate freely with each other gaining a better understanding of foreign cultures
- Globalization and technology raise language and cultural barriers
- The vast influx of information between countries gives all people more opportunities to learn and experience other cultures
- Globalization push the people of all countries to become more open to other cultures, ideas and traditions

- Globalization results in a loss of local culture and traditions as products and behaviors become truly global
- Manufacturing in one developing country may stimulate local economy, but it robs other countries of employment in the production sector
- With global trade, the rich are getting richer and the poor poorer
- Globalization is not working for the majority of the world, instead it is a great thing for owners and managers, but it is detrimental to workers and laborers leading to their exploitation

- Globalization makes it easier for companies and employers to act with less accountability exploiting workers, even children, to keep up with demand
- Labor Drain results in loss of job opportunities to local economies
- Skilled workers and professionals like doctors from poor countries are enticed to leave their own countries and migrate to areas with higher paying jobs
- Poor countries lose a large number of professionals who could have been of service to their own countries
- Workers of the host countries lose their jobs due to the fact that foreign employees are willing to accept lower wages
- Globalization may also have negative impact on the environment as the increased consumption of a wide variety of products leads to increased production resulting in more pollution and devastating long term effects on the planet's environmental stability
- Global trade and excess consumption may lead in more wastes to be produced and dumped with no regard for the environmental consequences in poorer countries

9.10. Cultural Globalization

Effects

- The world today has become a global village
- People in all corners of the world are increasingly exposed to similar services and products and adopt similar habits
- It can weaken national culture and traditions
- Watching films and television programs produced in the United States, may lead people adopt aspects of the lifestyle of the American characters they see on television
- The more habits, products and services we share, the better we understand each other and this reduces prejudice against other nations
- Modernity is a sign of progress in a society that people no longer are restricted to brands and advertisements from their own society but are able to access more international goods

10. Health

10.1. Free Access to Health Care

Opponents

- Health is the responsibility of the individual
- People should pay for their own health care, not have it given to them by the government
- Free access to health care should be paid through taxes, and as there are people who dot work hard, or at all, to pay the necessary taxes, it would force to subsidize free health care. This seems unfair for those who work hard and pay taxes
- Expanding free access to health care to all citizens without distinction will increase the country's debt and deficit
- Providing free access to health care could increase the wait time for medical services
- Free access to health care leads to longer wait times than private health insurance and as a consequence, beneficiaries have trouble obtaining necessary care
- Free access to health care would lead to rationing of medical services putting restrictions on health care provided such as controlling distribution, budgeting, price setting, and service restrictions as well
- Free access to health care that do not render the individual directly responsible for the costs of medical services they receive would cause people to overuse the health care resources wasting valuable resources (utilizing more health resources than necessary)
- Free access to health care necessitates the raise of taxes to subsidize the health service

Proponents/Supporters

- Health is a fundamental right and should be available to everyone without restrictions
- The founding documents (**declaration/constitution**) of almost every **country/state** declares the right to free access to health care
- The purpose of any state is to promote the general welfare of its people, and hence health care is a responsibility of the government
- Everyone should have access to health care services and none should suffer financial hardship when obtaining these services

- Good hospitals are governmental responsibility
- A healthy population is vital to national interests as it is crucial for economic productivity
- People with adequate health care are healthy and miss work less, allowing them to contribute more to the economy
- Instituting free access to health care could lower the overall cost of health care due to lowered administrative and prescription drug costs
- Providing governments all citizens free access to health care could save more peoples' lives, and people would live longer and happier

10.2. Obesity (mostly child obesity) is a Disease

Proponents/Supporters

- Obesity is considered a disease as it satisfies the corresponding definitions and criteria
- Obesity, like all other diseases, impairs the normal functioning of the body, its normal mobility, for example the range of motion in knees and hips. It is also linked to reproductive impairment, sexual dysfunction, infertility and risk of miscarriage in women, and lower sperm counts in men
- Obesity can be a genetic disorder that can be inherited like other personality traits
- Genetic disposition plays a large role in determining if a person will be obese or not

Opponents

- Obesity is not a disease itself, but a preventable risk factor for other diseases and conditions
- Obesity is not a disease but a side effect, caused by other diseases, certain drugs, even by lack of sleep, quitting smoking and many other factors
- Obesity is the result of eating too much. The body converts excess calories into fat
- Obesity is the result of sedentary lifestyles
- People today tend to spend more time commuting, sitting in front of a computer, watching television, playing video games, especially the younger generation, and generally exercising less

Reasons/Causes

- Junk food is a major factor in poor diet and this is detrimental to health
- Eating too much junk food can lead to health issues, as obesity, later in life
- Many people, especially young, eat fast food because they have a lifestyle that doesn't allow them to have time to sit down to a proper meal

- Burgers and pizzas are seen to be a cooler meal and young people prefer them in order to impress their peers
- There is a reliance today on the consumption of processed foods
- **Poor diet/unhealthy eating** habits when eating out
  - There is a large number of fast food restaurants available
  - The food in these places has been proven to be very unhealthy
  - Children constitute the bulk of the customers of these establishments, and much of the advertising concerning them is targeted at children
- **Poor diet/unhealthy eating** habits at home
  - Ready-made meals are a quick and easy option for parents who are working hard
  - A lot of food consumed at home is processed food, which have a high fat, salt and sugar content
  - A growing number of people eat irregularly and consume large portions of high-calorie food
- Poor fitness levels as a result of inactive lifestyle
- Inactive lifestyle leads to burning less calories and gaining weight
- More and more people
  - rely on cars instead of walking
  - have less physical demands at work
  - prefer inactive leisure activities

Effects

- Overweight people are very unhealthy and often suffer from stress and tiredness
- Overweight people are more likely to have serious illnesses such as diabetes and heart disease
- Physical health problems and loss of productivity are among the most serious diseases
- Obesity results in incorrect functioning of the human body and contributes to the risk of developing some chronic illnesses
- Increased body fat worsens the metabolism, which in turn may result in diabetes or heart diseases
- Many overweight children often experience bullying from other children affecting their mental health
- Obesity affect self-esteem and is deemed to be a (negative) stigma
- Health problems related to obesity and poor fitness can result in premature death decreasing life expectancy
- Obesity, and diseases stem from it, lessen work capacity, as obese people need to put more effort to complete some tasks than a person with normal weight

Solution

- Individuals/People
  - must take some responsibility for their diet and health

- o can change their diet and their physical activity increasing life expectancy and reducing the obesity levels
  - o could and should ensure that their diets are healthy and balanced, leading to a reduction in obesity levels
  - o could improve their fitness levels by choosing to walk or cycle to work or to the shops rather than taking the car and to walk up stairs instead of taking the lift
  - o must chose regular exercise that can prevent obesity and therefore reduce the risk of heart disease and stroke
  - o especially families should prepare their own foods, and consume more fruit and vegetables
  - o should adopt a balanced diet which includes foods from the five groups (proteins, carbohydrates, grains, dairy produce, and fats) with less emphasis on fats
- Parents are responsible for their children's diet and should provide them with meals that are nutritious encouraging them to avoid junk food and sugary snacks during the day
- Governments
  - o could implement educational programs to improve their citizens, and especially children's, eating and exercise habits
  - o should try to combat a wide range of social factors that cause people to eat unhealthily
  - o should add classes to the curriculum about healthy diet and lifestyles
  - o could also implement measures to encourage their citizens to walk or cycle instead of taking the car, as for example be building more cycle lanes or increasing vehicle taxes
  - o should regulate the ingredients of processed food
  - o could ban advertisements for unhealthy foods on television
  - o could spend more money on preventative measures, such as campaigns, to encourage exercise and a good diet
- Children who have learned in school about the need to have a varied and balanced diet with plenty of vitamins tend to eat more healthily, while in contrast, people who have not had this education still eat too much junk food

10.3. Banning Smoking

Proponents/Supporters

- People's health is more important than businesses, smoke businesses
- Governments have to carry huge financial burden because of smoking consequences on people's health
- The increased number of smokers who have health problems that are in need of medical treatment or hospitalization lead in increased cost which lies upon the tax payers

- Banning smoking could safe guard the general population's health from the well known effects of smoking
- Smoking has been proved to be harmful to health as it consist of many carcinogenic compounds which cause serious harm to health
- Research has shown that smokers are at a greater risk to develop serious health problems, such as heart disease and lung cancer, especially for people who have been smoking from a young age for a long period of time
- Smokers experience symptoms like shortness of breath, fatigue, or respiratory problems even on a daily basis
- Passive smoking has also adverse health effects
- Active smoking is not only unhealthy to the individual but also for society in general due to the effect of second-hand smoke which can be as damaging as active smoking
- Non-smokers who live close to smokers can develop cancers of the lungs, mouth, throat, and other sites in the body, or suffer other health problems as breathing disorder, if they spend long periods of time among people who do smoke
- A typical example of the passive smoking repercussions is the poor health of children growing up in a home where either one or both parents smoke
- To be exposed to other's people smoke (passive smoking) is a clear violation of non-smokers' rights
- Non-smokers have made the conscious choice to not expose themselves to the dangers this habit (smoking) entails, however, they cannot avoid been exposed to other's people smoke

Opponents

- Smoking is a matter of freedom of choice
- It is smokers' democratic right to smoke and this personal decision deserves to be respected
- In a democratic society, the freedom of choice also encompasses the right to engage in activities of one's preference, including the choice to smoke insofar as this does not infringe upon the rights of others (non-smokers)
- Smokers are aware of the implications of their habit and they have deliberately chosen to smoke, despite the health risks involved
- Some smokers are addicted and suffer if they do not have the opportunity to smoke a cigarette occasionally
- Passive smokers make the choice to breathe in other people's smoke by going to places where smoking is allowed
- If passive smokers would prefer not to smoke passively, then they do not need to visit places where smoking is permitted
- Banning smoking would possibly drive many bars and pubs out of business as smokers would not go there anymore
- The smoking industry provides a considerable amount of income for governments via taxation

- Smoking industry contributes towards the general economy as well as paying for some of the damage that smoking causes through taxation
- High taxation or any other limits on smoking industry's product would result in the loss of jobs or the collapse of the industry as a whole
- If smoking should be restricted (banning smoking) in most public areas, it would probably result in more and more smokers decide to give up smoking reducing this way the state income via smoking taxes

- Bars could allow smoking, but clearly indicate this at the entrance of the establishment so as to non-smokers bothered by smoke could choose not to visit them often/frequent
- Specially designated smoking areas could be arranged in airports and other public places

10.4. Food Additives

- The use of food colorings improves the products to the eye encouraging people to purchase food that may otherwise not look tempting to eat
- Using food preservatives help products to have longer shelf life
- Much of the food we eat would not actually last long if it were not for chemicals they contain (food preservatives, additive that preserves food)
- Food companies claim these food additives are safe and there are researches that support this

- There is not much research as to how far these chemicals are safe
- The research is being made by the food companies or people with connections to these companies and, therefore, they are quite possibly biased
- There are many reports nowadays published in the press about possible links of food additives to various health issues such as cancer
- Food additives have been linked to problems such as hyperactivity in children
- The advantages are to the companies that sell food and not to the customer

10.5. Alternative Medicine

- Alternative medicine cannot be without any positive effect as many people are willing to pay considerable sums for alternative treatments, whilst conventional medicine is available without charge
- There is a lot of anecdotal evidence to suggest that these therapies work
- These therapies are far from being dangerous
- They often have few or no side effects
- At the worst outcome there would be no change

- There is little scientific research into such medicine
- There is a scarcity of evidence to support the claims of their proponents
- Part of the reason for the successfulness of this kind of cure may be that people come to the therapist with a very positive attitude
- Alternative Medicine may be only useful for long-term, chronic conditions
- Acute medical problems often require more conventional methods

11. Education

11.1. Self-Study, Long Distance Learning, and New Learning-Technology

For

- Learning through self-study (e.g. a foreign language) allows for flexibility in terms of schedule, as it is not essential for students to be present in the lecture theatre for their courses
- Self-Study allows the studying time to be arranged according to student's daily needs and responsibilities
- Through self-study students do not have to conform to the program of, e.g. a language institute
- Self-Study promotes the development of autonomous learning
- Self-Study or distance learning is ideal for part-time courses for adults who are in employment
- Distance learning courses is appropriate for people from other countries
- Using new technology, lecturers and tutors have the opportunity to use advanced tools, such as interactive whiteboards, to deliver their courses in a more stimulating way and to large numbers of students

Against

- Teachers have a sensitivity to students' individual needs and thus can adapt themselves to a wide variety of different kind of students and classes
- Technology is not able to attain such a sensitivity so that understand students' needs
- Strong effort despite intellectual weakness, cannot be perceived nor dealt with by a computer
- Traditional educational system involves students' interaction who learn to communicate, cooperate and often compromise with other classmates
- Students' interaction is an aspect completely lacking in a self-study or education using exclusively technological means
- Education is a human activity and it works best with as much human interaction as possible
- Impersonal technology cannot replace the human contact found in traditional face-to-face tutorials and seminars

- Self-teaching can result in lacking certain, and essential skills, as unsupervised learners may focus too much on one part of the subject and neglect other important parts. For example, memorizing grammar rules, or focus too much on vocabulary lists, or pay insufficient attention to using the language for written or oral communication, when learning a foreign language
- With self-teaching, students will achieve only part of the desired results, e.g. be able to translate the new language but not to use it in interactive contexts

11.2. Compulsory Education until 18

For

- The time spent at school is fundamental for normal mental development
- Children's development into healthy adults is the primary purpose of any education and therefore education should be mandatory up to the end of adolescence
- The period between five and eighteen years of any human is a crucial stage in their life cycle
- Young people need guidance to gain social responsibility too
- In school students
  - increase their level of self-sufficiency
  - acquire a sense of self-esteem
  - develop feelings of personal empowerment
  - are encouraged to think independently
  - take responsibility for their actions
  - interacting with peers
  - feel part of the school community
  - become disciplined individuals who obey rules
  - become strong, well-rounded individuals
  - develop cooperative skills
  - gain both basic and specialized knowledge necessary for their adult life, regardless of what their vocation may be
  - progress smoothly from childhood to adolescence and finally, adulthood
- School
  - imparts wisdom and moral values
  - aims at raising social awareness
  - trains students for their future careers
  - promotes career as education is needed for skilled work
  - promotes respect for others
  - encourages students to be active members of society
  - provides a platform to acquire a sense of belonging
  - provides moral and social education too
- Staying in school until the age of 18
  - Prepares young people for working career

- o The education received between the ages of 16 and 18 is crucial for skilled work
  - o Young people tend to be more responsible and help build a stronger society
  - o Society gain also from the contribution graduates can make to the economy
- Leaving school earlier than 18, student
  - o get only the basic education
  - o remain unskilled, and as a consequence it is more unlikely to be able to find any skilled work

- Children are not able to absorb so much information the school can provide
- Some people benefit more from vocational training than academic education
- Some professions need vocational training or apprenticeships
- In today's world, young people are maturing in ever earlier age, and are able to make their own life decisions by the age of 16

11.3. Free Higher Education

- Everyone should have the right to get educated and the equal opportunity to free higher education fulfils this right
- Countries with academic educated population have higher levels of innovation and productivity
- Educating more people, society can benefit as it leads to a more productive and educated workforce
- Education is a very important commodity that equips people who receive it with abilities useful even for society and not only for them
- Low income students may be dissuaded from attending university or even be excluded from these institutions, as they may not be able to secure the financial support of their studies from their family. This may be considered unfair and a clear form of discrimination
- As universities grow in size, higher education is getting expensive and they cannot resort to students' payments/ fees to maintain standards and ensure the quality of the teaching
- University Education secures a better job and improves peoples' possibilities to future career prospects
- Higher University Education increases a person's marketable skills and attractiveness to potential employers

- Education is a precious commodity and should be paid for by its recipients, the students
- If all people would receive higher education then it would be a shortage of people available to do manual jobs, thus making university expensive may encourage people to take up these jobs
- Students who pay for their studies generally study harder than those who get free access to education

11.4. Studying Abroad

Reasons

- Universities abroad may provide courses that are more in line with the students' interests and may have better facilities
- Studying abroad enable students to experience a culture different to what they were used to
- More people are affluent enough
- There is a variety of grants and scholarships available for overseas students
- It is sometimes a matter of necessity as in some countries, places in institutions of higher learning are limited and competition for these places is fierce
- Many leading universities abroad are renowned for their high educational standards
- Many leading universities abroad are often well funded, able to offer students a range of benefits, such as a wider choice of subjects and more high-tech facilities

Benefits

- Studying abroad can offer students the opportunity to improve their knowledge of a second language, and to get used to live and work in a different cultural environment
- Living on your own when you are student is a very positive experience as it offers independence and help young people become more responsible
- Young people can enjoy their student life to the full, only when they spend some years living in another place away from home gain unforgettable experiences
- Leaving families and living with other student together, or on they own, give students the opportunity to meet new friends, develop better social skills and improve their character
- Students' maturity and confidence grow better and faster when they live alone and forcing them take care of themselves, enabling them to live more fulfilling lives

- The independence, that the living away from home entails, develops social skills, improves personality, grows maturity and confidence
- The sense of independence when living alone and study in another place away from home provides students with the opportunity to experience new things and stand on their own feet
- Studying abroad gives students access to knowledge and facilities such as laboratories and libraries which are not available in their home country
- Abroad students find a wider range of courses than those offered in their country's universities
- Abroad offered courses and programs may fit more closely to students particular requirements
- Abroad students became highly desirable to prospective employers

Drawbacks/Problems

- Changing living environment can be quite stressful and affect students personality
- When leaving home to go to study, students miss their support network of family and old friends
- Newly-arrived students may feel uncertainty, confusion, homesickness, and being out of place
- Student studying in another country may face a breakdown in communication, as there may be language obstacle/barrier due to their lack of fluency in the language spoken in the new country
- Newly-arrived students need to adjust quickly to the foreign mentality and completely new culture to overcome these problems
- Students have to leave their family and friends for a long period
- Studying abroad is almost always more expensive that studying in one's local university
- Students who study abroad often have to study in a foreign language

Solutions

- Students should
  - have an active attitude and take sufficient precautions
  - **improve /strive to enrich** their language skills by taking some courses before going abroad
  - enlarge their circle of friends
  - join some societies
  - keep an open attitude towards the new culture

11.5. Formal Examinations

- They have been designed to be objective measures of the students ability or proficiency in a particular subject
- They are a fair system as everyone has an equal opportunity since they all sit the same exam at the same time
- They provide a clear and objective measure of what students have learned
- Those who work hard can expect to be rewarded with a high grade
- They are an excellent way of motivating learners to study harder and to reward the students who do best
- It is difficult to cheat if the exam is properly invigilated
- Examinations test the ability of students to work under pressure, and this is a vital life skill for their later careers
- Formal examinations are objective, a motivation to study, and a preparation for life
- Though formal examination is not the only method of **judging/ascertaining** what has been achieved, it is widely used as the only practically sufficient way on a large scale
- They provide a clear and objective measure of what students have learned, whereas any form of continuous assessment is probably going to be far more subjective

Cons/Against

- They are the number one anxiety producer as the passing or failing determines what happens next
- Anxiety generates more anxiety and as result the fear of failure may lead students to break down
- Failing create fear of losing face among our peers
- The psychological factor play a role in approaching important examinations and affects the corresponding results
- Focusing only on formal exams, important components of students' development may not be considered as important by teachers and students may not be treated accordingly
- Exams are an inappropriate way of measuring students' performance and should be replaced by continuous assessment
- Some students naturally excel in exams, whereas others find it difficult to work under these stressful and time-constrained conditions and, may not, therefore, always reflect their true ability
- Continuous assessment is a more effective way of testing subjects such as design and technology, which are more creative and less academic

- Continuous assessment can allow teachers to reward students who work hard, but who may be less able and not do well in more formal testing
- Continuous assessment could be more appropriate to relieve the students of exam pressure and to measure their abilities, especially in lower age groups where young children can be affected negatively by stress and under-perform in exams

11.6. Continuous Examination

For/Pros

- Allows those students who work at a slower pace to take more time to work on their course work and projects
- Teachers can observe and assist students who may be weaker providing them with the opportunity to improve during the education period
- Continuous examination through projects encourage team work, an important skill that is necessary for future employment
- This is more suitable for occasions where it would be better to relieve the students of exam pressure and to measure their abilities through continuous assessment
- It is a more effective way of testing subjects such as design and technology, that are more creative and less academic
- It can allow teachers to reward students who work hard, but who may be less able to do well in more formal testing

Cons/Against

- Any form of continuous assessment is probably to be far more subjective than formal examinations

Dealing with examinations

- Student must learn to
  - recognize panic and take a deep breath to calm down
  - slow down and give themselves time to understand what they are asked to do
  - look after themselves so that they can be as fresh as possible, mentally and physically
  - isolate themselves from the negative thoughts and concentrate on their tasks and goals

For/Pros

- It is more possible to get a good job if you know at least one foreign language
- Modern technology has made the world smaller and, therefore, communication skills are essential
- Being able to communicate with people in other countries is very important in the modern world, and we need to speak different languages in order to do this

Way to learning a foreign language

- Most people choose to enroll in a private language school
- A good language school offers teachers who are native speakers of the language you are learning
- Other people prefer private tuitions that
    o involves no travelling, no sharing lesson time with other students
    o are often much more effective
    However
    o they are expensive, costing, in general, more than group learning
    o and student miss the social aspect of the classroom

11.8. Learning a Foreign Languages in the earliest grades

For/Pros

- To learn a foreign language well, it is best to start in childhood, as childhood is the best time to learn foreign languages
- Children are eager to absorb new information
- Children can learn to speak foreign languages as well as their native language
- It is difficult to learn a foreign language well if you start studying it at a later age
- The best way to learn a foreign language is to start studying it during the first years of school

Reasons

- Teachers may lack the ability to discipline students
- There have been cases were pupils have sued teachers for disciplining them too harshly
- Children are aware of the fact that there are limits to what a teacher can do and they take advantage of this constrain without respect and do not concentrate if they do not want to
- The diet of children affects their behavior: additives in snacks and carbonated drinks can cause hyperactivity and a lack of ability to concentrate in class

Solutions

- Though it is obvious that children should not be abused, teachers should be given more power to use any appropriate method to control the class without fear of recrimination
- Schools' canteens and parents must provide children with healthy food, not snacks containing a lot of additives
- Separating out problematic students will result in quieter and more orderly classrooms. The majority of children benefit and learn better as this enables students to learn more effectively and without distraction
- Separating out problematic students the rest of them no longer are distracted by classmates who either talk all the time, or ignore the teacher, and the teachers are able to concentrate on instructing their students and do not waste time on disciplinary matters
- However, there may be practical problems in implementing this policy since
  - Disruptive students placed in special classes may behave even worse than before when they are put together with normal children
  - There is less chance of badly behaved children to improve when they do not have the positive influence of well-behaved classmates
  - Special classes become unmanageable and cause even more problems than they try to solved

12. Free Time Activities

Benefits

- Offers considerable financial benefits for the residents
- **Boosts/stimulates** local economy
- **Generates income/increases the income** of local businesses, such as supermarkets, souvenir shops, restaurants or cafes
- Brings new money (valuable foreign exchange) in local economies that can support community facilities and services that otherwise might not be developed
- The tourism industry provides plenty of job opportunities
- Creates local jobs and business opportunities
- The unemployment rates tend to be low in touristic areas
- Provides cultural exchange between hosts and guests
- Facilities and infrastructure developed for tourism can also be used by the residents benefiting them
- Fosters the development of new skills and the learning of new languages

Drawbacks

- Local residents get disturbed due to the vast number of tourists
- Mass tourism may threaten specific natural resources such as beaches, or historical sites
- May increase litter, noise, and pollution, as popular tourist locations are swamped by tourists
- Construction of huge hotel complexes etc., may destroy local environment and animal habitats
- Brings increased competition for limited resources such as water and land, resulting in land degradation, loss of wildlife habitats and deterioration of scenery
- Emissions generated by transport means are one of the main environmental problems (pollution) cause by tourism
- May create crowding and congestion
- May inflate property values and prices of goods and services

- Employment tends to be seasonal and workers may be laid off in the winter season
- Many jobs in the tourism industry are poorly paid

12.2. Ecotourism

Pros

- Local people benefit from ecotourism in the same way as in the ordinary tourism
- Less fortunate places can benefit most
- Money from ecotourism helps to preserve wildlife
- It provides sustainable income for local communities and incentives for environmental protection
- It gives people the opportunity to have a new experience with nature, learn about environmental problems and the importance of preserving natural habitats

Cons

- Only foreign investors and corporations benefit from ecotourism, not local communities
- Ecotourism can damage the areas it wants to protect and ruin natural habitats as highly visited ecotourism destinations is more likely to undergo habitat fragmentation and destruction, leading to loss of species

12.3. Attracting More Tourists

Pros/Advantages

- It will bring in large amounts of foreign currency
- Visitors will spend money on accommodation, entertainment and souvenirs, which is an excellent way to improve the local economy
- Local hotel and restaurant owners, as well as manufacturers and crafts people, would financially
- Existing hotel and entertainment facilities should be improved and modernized by spending more money
- This will attract more tourists to the region and at the same time, provide extra opportunities for employment for local residents, especially young people
- An increase in tourism would lead to a rise in the standard of living for the local population
- Local people would take advantage of the facilities provided for visitors, such as improved transport services and leisure activities
- The horizons of local people would be widened through their contact with various cultures from other countries

- Information about local historical buildings, archeological sites, the town's museum, should be made available and accessible by an eye-catching website created in several languages to ensure that these attractions are brought to the notice of a wide audience
- Local historians be invited to write leaflets with interesting facts and anecdotes about these places

12.4. Travelling

Pros/Benefits

- Traveling is educational and can open our eyes and mind in a way we could never thought possible
- Travelling broadens the mind (makes people more open-minded) as it offers a window on the world
- Through travel, we can become more aware of the world around us
- It allows people to experience different cultures and locations
- Traveling provides the opportunity to discover other cultures, foods and traditions
- Visiting different places provides people the opportunity to come into contact with the cultures and traditions of various nations and get familiarized with different lifestyles and mentalities
- Travel is a learning experience as we can see other parts of the world and get acquainted with foreign cultures
- Travel allows people to escape from their problems and reconsider their lives, their relationships, or their job
- Travelling allows us to see our lives from a fresh perspective
- Traveling represents an important physiological need to break normal routine, the job you hate, or simply a boring, sedentary life
- Travelling is an unmatched form of recreation that add excitement to our lives and alleviate boredom
- International travel creates ties between nations and develops positive attitudes towards people of other countries and cultures

Cons

- Traveling can be costly and unaffordable, or even extremely expensive, as many tourist countries have incredibly high costs of living
- Traveling may be addictive and never enough, especially if you are prone to becoming addicted to things that please you, turning it into an incurable sense of restlessness that cannot be satisfied

- Travel can be challenging if you are unfamiliar with the language, customs and cuisine of the destination country

- Package vacations provide all-inclusive package deals with a range of **bars/restaurants/stores** nearby, extensive entertainment facilities on hand, along with childcare facilities
- Package vacations tend to be cheaper in general, because many operators can make deals with airlines and hoteliers that arranging a similar booking by yourself cannot
- As flights, accommodation, and maybe meals and transport are paid **in advance/upfront**, prices are considerably lower and more affordable
- In package holidays you are protected by law in cases the travel or the airline company bankrupts, you will be refunded if you are already traveling, and entitled to **hotel costs/flights home** if you are abroad
- Package holidays are unstressed and remove much of the burden and computer rage that comes with planning a holiday (e.g. price comparisons)
- Families - Package holidays are often advantageous as many tour operators organize kids' activities
- Package resorts usually have a tour operator representative on the ground dealing with requests, excursions or emergencies
- Some companies allow customers to customize their own package, which gives them the option to exclude superfluous activities and offers
- Package holidays are convenient as everything have been taken care for you and all you have to worry about is how to relax and enjoy your holiday for the most
- When you take a tour, someone else handles all the details. You choose an itinerary, pay the tour operator and let the professionals deal with airlines, drivers, guides, and hotels. All you need to do is arrive at your departure point on time
- With package holidays you have access to unusual or overcrowded destinations, as tour operators set up trips to just about anywhere, even to places most individuals cannot reach on their own
- Tour groups have their own access times and entrances, and do not stand in line saving time as it is usually limited
- Package holidays use tour guides which is especially important when you are visiting a place for the first time

- Package holidays often mean compromising. For example, full-board meal requires you to dine in the hotel restaurant every night rather than in a local restaurant
- Package holidays are suitable only for standard length vacations, usually a week or a fortnight
- Package holidays are not for those who prefer to see things at their own pace and like the flexibility the independent travel provides
- In package holidays there is often a lack of free time, as many tour itineraries do not include enough free time and you are only limited to a few hours here and there
- In package holidays you have not any control on your accommodations and dining options as hotel and restaurant choices have been made by the travel agent
- In package holidays personality conflicts are possible among package takers
- All inclusive does not always mean all inclusive and a lot of things can be left out which means that they must be covered by you
- In package holidays most people are restricted to their all-inclusive hotels, since they do not want to spend more, and as a result, they rarely explore the host country or go for excursions
- The money you spend purchasing a package holiday may not support the local economy as they end up in international hotel chains and not the local economy
- In package holidays you may visit too touristy and overcrowded **overdeveloped resorts/mass tourism destinations** in multi-storey hotels
- As you are often restricted by set mealtimes your exposure to local culture is minimal

12.6. Camping Vacations

Pros/Advantages

- It offers great mobility and flexibility
- It allows vacations for those on a tight budget
- It is cheap and cheerful and gives you the opportunity to be back to nature and not feeling tied to technology
- Many campsites are more affordable than hotel rooms
- Provide you with ample space to accommodate friends and family as there are many modern campground equipped with amenities
- Many campsites can accommodate multiple tents, which means you can camp with your friends in the same site
- Greater storage capacity for gear
- You can enjoy being woken up by the sun and heading to bed late in the night
- You can have a BBQ any time you want even more than once in the same day
- Kids can play outside all day and make new friendships

- You can enjoy the fresh air and silence

- Many campgrounds provide only basic amenities
- There are only communal showers and toilets available and you have to share them with the other campers
- You have to carry heavy camping gear
- The storage and maintenance costs of the camping equipment can be high
- Campers are dependent on weather, especially in a tent, and bugs, heat, rain, and wind can all impact how comfortable your camping trip is
- Sleeping in a tent on the ground with a sleeping pad is less comfortable than in hotel on your bed
- Cooking, as well as many other activities, will be conducted outside

13. Working Life

Pros of young people

- Younger people are more able to understand technology and they are instantly able to make the most of the technology at their disposal
- Working with much information, numbers and calculations, to be young is often an advantage
- Certain jobs (high-tech industries such as computer programming) are more suited to a younger person owning to their physical and mental state
- Younger employees are adept at technology as they have grown up in this era and are therefore much more proficient at it than the older generation
- They are more risk-taking and more open to the new idea
- They display more flexibility than older employees who tend to have their own set of ideas and notions and cannot adapt easily to a changing mindset
- Their expectation of salary is low and therefore they save companies budged

Cons of young people

- Younger employees may never have had any actual experience in the real business world before
- New workers' straight of college require constant care as well as attention in their first few months of work
- Younger people often tend to be a little rowdy in the work place
- Young employees do not usually know what is expected of them in a formal setting as opposed to an older person
- Younger people are more confused about what they should do, causing them to make more mistakes

Pros of older people

- Older workers are more reliable, respectful, have a more responsible attitude, and a stronger work ethic
- Older worker have experience to back up their job since they have probably worked in another company before
- They do not require any training, in contrast to new employees as they know what to do

- They already knows how to conduct themselves in a formal situation
- They have a more mature manner of dealing with difficult issues
- They probably make fewer errors as they probably have already made mistakes and hopefully learned from them
- Older employees are able to guide the newer employees based on their experiences (successes or failures) they have obtained in the past
- Experienced employees have a greater and clear understanding of the business world
- They usually tend to be more conscientious and even more responsible when it comes to carrying out tasks which have been entrusted to them
- The older person tend to have a more in depth knowledge of the business world than any youth
- They are more able to and more experienced in applying their theoretical knowledge and putting it into practice
- Older employees have invaluable work experience, including diverse thoughts and approaches
- Older employees are usually more able to mentor younger, less-experienced employees, as they display more patience to teach and to communicate with them
- Older employees have a serious commitment to work, and they are loyal

Cons of older people

- They probably are too set in their way of working and therefore they are unable to change and keep up with the pace and demands of the modern world
- They may believe that they do not need any instruction and follow the dictates of their own minds
- The older people may not be able to use **modern technology/the state of the art technology** well which companies might need
- Generally, among older worker there is no sense of competition, as they are usually satisfied with their job
- Older people tend to like to do everything manually, without the use of technology, which sometimes is an incredible waste of time
- They may not be able to adapt themselves to new setting
- They may be near to the age of retirement and they will not any more work after a short period of time
- Sometimes older employees, as older people do, may not be open to criticism, while younger people are more eager workers
- They have a lack of flexibility as mature employees tend to be more rigid and less flexible
- Mature workers tend to have, or require, the more senior positions within an organization, so they are likely to command a higher salary compared to the younger generation
- Older workers sometimes find it difficult to cope with change in the technology and takes time to develop IT skills

- In older employees the absence of competition leads to lower productivity

13.2. Working while Studying

Supporters

- The parents of many students are not wealthy enough to afford their children' education
- With part time job students earn money and are financially independent
- Many students are independent from their families and are not supported from them economically
- Part-time jobs contribute to students' financial position, as they can partially support themselves
- In countries with high tuition fees, a part-time job is the essential factor in making students able to pay for their tuition fees and permitting study
- Intelligent but poor students cannot pursuit their study as they cannot financially support it
- Part-time jobs prepare a person for the real world of work what study cannot do
- Students can apply their theoretical study to practice
- Work experience gained during study can facilitate most people to develop their career
- Working while studying enhances students' interpersonal skills and leadership putting them in a favorable position in the future job markets

Opponents

- Part-time jobs would occupy a huge amount of time that student would require to devote to study
- Most jobs are merely basic work that might not promote specific students' skills
- Working while studying causes negative effects on study, with terrible consequences
- The primary purpose of students is to concentrate on their academic work, and if they are working they may not be able to devote themselves sufficiently to their study
- Working students do not have enough time for study, fail to meet the requirements of universities (attendance, performance, assignments, or exams), and have greater difficulty in passing their courses

Pros

- Being the owner of a company offers independence and autonomy as it allows you to
    - create the company's vision
    - set up the objectives for the business
    - determine the strategies
    - use your creativity and ingenuity to realize goals
    - be free to arrange your schedule as you **choose/wish**
    - decide what risks are worth taking in your businesses
    - choose who to hire and on what terms
- Entrepreneurs are not restricted or ordered around by others (e.g. superiors), as they are at the top of the pyramid
- Entrepreneurs with shrewdness, willingness to work tirelessly and a certain amount of luck can become extremely wealthy
- Being an entrepreneur allows you to enjoy a sense of fulfillment by seeing your efforts bear fruit, and watching your company expand

Cons

- The time required to run a successful business is huge and most entrepreneurs must often sacrifice family, personal life and freedom, in general
- Any sense of independence gained from being the boss may be lost due to the total commitment that is demanded
- Stress levels can become incredibly high, because employees must be paid and obligations fulfilled, regardless of the amount of profits
- There is no guarantee that any endeavor will be successful, no matter how much time and effort is put into it

13.4. Being an (star) actor/ actress

Pros/Advantages

- When success comes, it is very high

Cons/Disadvantages

- Only natural exhibitionists may love all the media attention
- You need to be able to deal with a life in the public eye
- You have to be prepared to sacrifice your privacy
- It affects your friends and family too

- You have to work hard to be a successful actor (However, this is true whatever job you choose to do)
- It may not be a steady job (working in a steady job you can enjoys security and peace of mind and look forward to a pension at the end of it)
- Years of effort may be rewarded with complete failure

It depends on the individual's character as to whether or not it is a worthwhile profession to follow

13.5. Unemployment

Causes

- Automation, the prevalence of computers and advanced technology resulted in fewer people to be required in certain fields
- Banking through ATM's rather than waiting in line for the bank teller has lead to many bank workers to be dismissed
- As people live longer, retirement ages increase, leaving fewer vacancies for the younger people
- Youths often pursue studies, usually motivated by ideas of prestige or status, paying little attention to the demands of the market, and as a result they are not competitive in the job market

Solutions

- Governments should motivate entrepreneurs to create new job vacancies
- Shortening of the working week may help more employees be hired by a company
- However, if a company was forced to employ more workers to produce the same amount of goods, then its wage bill would rise and its products might become more expensive and less competitive compared to companies with longer working weeks
- This way, the company either might become insolvent or it would have to make some employees redundant
- Moreover, the intended benefit to the personnel would not happen
- Reduction of the retirement age, creates positions vacancies for younger members of the workforce
- Proper dissemination of information among high school and university students would force them to seek careers in areas where more jobs are available

14. Sports

14.1. Team Sport

Advantages

- Children acquire social skills
- Each sport team is like a small community where rewarding experiences are shared among its members
- Being a team member involves cooperating with teammates as well as trusting them
- In group sport children learn to share the glory of victory as well as the pain of defeat
- Team sports instill discipline in children
- Children's self-improvement and building of new skills is fostered owning to the competition and solidarity
- In group sports weaker players can get inspired from the observation and emulation of the performances of stronger teammates
- The dynamics within teams can motivate the youngsters play in the spirit of competition and cooperation
- Playing team sports children get a lot of exercise, which is important for their physical and mental health
- They learn important skills such as teamwork, dealing with defeat, and winning graciously
- They can have a lot of fun

Disadvantages

- Some children who are not strong players may lag behind the others or even become dependent on them instead of developing individual strength
- These children may find it difficult to be compared to others. This may damage their self-esteem creating feelings of inferiority
- Differences between strong and weak teammates may result in friction between them and this tension may discourage younger players from cooperating with one another
- Team sports are not the only way to gain these benefits
- Team sports are not the only way to learn to work with others
- Children have opportunities to work on teams at school and with clubs or organizations

- Many children enjoy individual activities such as hiking or biking
- These sports are as healthy and as much fun for children as team sports

14.2. Sedentary Life – Inactive Lifestyle

Reasons

- Many people stay less active because they use cars instead of walking
- The majority of people prefer passive rest to workouts in the gym

Effects

- In physical inactivity, spine disorders, posture and backbone problems are more possible to occur
- Long periods of physical inactivity raise a risk of becoming overweight
- Inactive life causes people to burn fewer calories and easily gain weight
- Sitting too much may cause a decrease in skeletal muscle mass
- People living a sedentary life lose muscle tissue and develop curve spine, resulting in numerous spinal diseases experienced most frequently as backache
- Physical inactivity may contribute to anxiety and depression
- Physical inactivity is linked to high blood pressure, elevated cholesterol levels, and has been shown to be a risk factor for certain cardiovascular diseases, obesity and various spine disorders

Solution

- An active lifestyle can significantly reduce the chances of chronic health conditions, mental health disorders, and premature death
- People should choose regular physical activity and exercising by going to gyms
- Get up and go for running, or take a walk, or take the stairs instead the elevator
- Authorities should promote increasing the level of physical activity
- Authorities should promote an active lifestyle by advertising walking and cycling as safe and attractive alternatives to motorized transport

14.3. Hosting an International Sporting Event

For

- Costs involved are worthwhile as the country will be the centre of the sporting world for a long time period
- The honor and prestige for the host country is beyond any price and many people need a national pride

- In general, any international sporting event raises the profile of sports in the country
- It is also good for the local and regional tourism and attracts international investments
- It is a way to improve the infrastructure by building, for example, new housing and developing new transport networks
- The authorities can use the occasion of the sporting event to finance public works that will benefit the whole population in the long term
- The build infrastructure, stadia and arenas, is a sporting legacy for future generations
- The village for the athletes can be transformed into public housing and the various stadia can be used to build a sporting legacy for future generations

Against

- Hosting international sporting events brings more problems than benefits
- The cost to build new arenas and modernize the existing infrastructure, so that it can cater for the athletes and the spectators, is huge
- There are hidden costs, such as policing, that cannot be pre-calculated
- Usually the stadia are empty after the games
- There is urgent need for investment in other areas such as health
- The money spent in sport infrastructure would be better spent on welfare and education programs that provide direct support for the population
- There is always present the possible problem of debt
- Some governments have incurred so much debt through hosting the Olympic Games that they have had to reduce spending on other social programs

15. Social and Cultural Issues

15.1. Euthanasia

For

- It provides a way to relieve extreme pain and give a death with dignity
- It provides a way of relief when a person's quality of life is low
- An agreement to requests for a quick end could be considered more compassionate
- It would be a relief for family and friends who witness the patient suffering
- Terminally-ill patient suffer unbearably which is inhuman
- It frees up medical funds to help other people
- Everyone has the right to control the destiny of their life
- It is another case of freedom of choice
- Persons being sick on bed are at the mercy of nurses, medical staff, and family for things like eating, using the restroom, changing clothes, and bathing

Against

- Euthanasia devalues human life and is in fact physician-assisted suicide
- For a wide range of reasons, relatives may often put pressure on depressed or financially-dependant people to accept euthanasia
- If pain and depression are adequately treated the desire to commit suicide disappears
- The term terminally-ill is difficult to define as some people who have been diagnosed as terminally-ill have lived on for years
- Euthanasia can become a means of health care cost containment
- The tremendous costs involved in the care of terminally ill patients or patients in a coma could prompt hospitals and doctors to use euthanasia as a means of money saving

- Newly-arrived people need to adjust quickly to the foreign mentality and completely new culture in order to be productive and able to be integrated in the society
- Poor command of the language makes it difficult for immigrants to be accepted by the host community leading to psychological problems, culture shock, and maybe to financial difficulties
- Immigrants often have difficulty finding work due to the competitive job markets
- When understood that there are difficulties in finding stable, legal employment (much trickier than anticipated), it results in great disappointment
- Foreigners take jobs and cause unemployment among the displaced indigenous workers
- Host cultures are often hostile to immigrants, and they met racist treatment
- Foreigners strain social service budgets

Solutions

- Governments of the host countries should providing accessible information for immigrants
- Immigrants should be prepared before leaving their own country having obtained qualifications in fields which are in demand in the country of relocation
- Host countries should organize affordable language courses for immigrants especially for those who are in need of assistance
- Immigrants improve the labor situation by creating new jobs and bringing valuable technical skills and knowledge with them

15.3. Spending Public Money on Arts

Supporters

- It is difficult for many arts institutions to generate much profit
- Without help from the government, many art places, like theaters, would have to close
- The arts have important impact on the quality of life
- Most people get great pleasure seeing music and theatre performances

- Public services, such as hospitals, roads and schools, are more important in maintaining life standards and should be supported first instead of arts
- Without enough money on hospitals, the health of our society may decline
- Schools need economic support or else our children may not be properly educated
- If public services are not subsidized the poor, the most vulnerable social group, would suffer more because they are more dependent on such services

15.4. Spending Public Money on Preserving the Past

For

- Preserving our national cultural heritage is important as it can teach us about our past
- It is important to protect the most famous sites for the future generations
- If our cultural heritage get lost, it is lost forever
- Caring for important monuments helps knowing and remembering the past
- Building and maintaining museums and keeping historic sites in good condition attract tourists, which has an economic benefit for everyone

Against

- We should look forwards and not backwards, spending less money on preserving the past and more on securing our future
- Poor people need houses to live in
- Businesses need better roads for transporting their goods
- Altering heritage sites to make them attractive for tourists by putting on entertainment gives a very untrue picture of the past and sometimes damages the local environment
- It is not realistic to try and save everything. Instead, we need to invest in the future too.

15.5. Addictions

Forms

- Drug addition
- Alcoholism
- Chain smoking
- Compulsive gambling
- Uncontrolled computer gaming etc.

- Prolonged drug dependence interferes with every organ in the human body
- More deaths, illnesses, and disabilities are caused by substance abuse than by any other preventable health condition
- Drugs damage the immune system, and a weakened immune system increases the risk of illness and the susceptibility to infection
- Common symptoms: nausea, vomiting, abdominal pain, changes in appetite and weight loss
- Drugs use may cause widespread brain damage that can interfere with memory, problems, attention and decision-making, as well as permanent brain damage, making daily living more difficult
- A person with drug addiction believes that they can deal with problems only after having taken drug
- Injected drugs may lead to heart/ cardiovascular conditions ranging from abnormal heart rates to heart attacks and collapsed veins and blood vessel infections
- Another possible consequence is the creation of increased strain on the liver, which puts the person at risk of significant liver damages, liver overexertion, or liver failure
- Drugs use leads into damaging the users social and emotional well-being, such as loss of employment, relationship loss, incarceration/ imprisonment, financial trouble, homelessness, risky sexual behavior

- Generally speaking, people start using drugs to escape or mask pain
- In some individuals, the drug use stem from untreated psychiatric issues including anxiety and depression
- The use of drugs can provide temporary solace/consolation from suffering
- Most addictions may stem from mental health issues including:
  - Trauma or abuse
  - Mental illness
  - Low self-esteem
  - Poverty
  - Relationship problems
  - Loss of a loved one
  - Stress
  - Chronic pain or medical conditions

15.6. Living Alone

Pros

- At the end of a long hectic day, you can come to a quiet and peaceful house and enjoy the silence, making it the perfect place for you to relax and unwind
- Living alone allows people to experience and even enjoy some sort of calmness and silence in their life
- Living alone provides complete and total privacy for doing anything you want without worrying about what other people, e.g. roommates, will say
- Every person living alone faces a level of independence in their life and lives the way they always wanted
- Living alone can definitely provide to a person complete freedom and independence without external control over their life
- Living alone allows people to host events at their place or arrange parties at any time they desire
- You can invite friends to stay in your house with you for a few days or even organize a party without the need to consult with roommates before
- There are no rules, not any interference from anyone. You have your inner peace and freedom of designing your own life as none can tell you what to do and what not to do
- You have no roommate altercations that **make you get upset/ become distressed** due to any of your habits
- You can decorate your room based on your preferences and nobody can interfere
- You can leave and return whenever you want, without having to worry about any issue
- Living alone gives you the opportunity to keep as many pets as you want unless the apartment regulation allows to keep pets
- Living alone allows you to keep your things as clean as you may want, or at any place you want and no one will come in to mess with your things
- There are no cleaning issues, the most common problem a person can face when living with other roommates or fellow mates, as they only have to clean up the mess of one person
- You can sleep or eat anywhere in your house, listen to any type of music you want, and there is no need to share anything
- You never have to wait to use the bathroom or be concerned about hot water usage
- There is nobody to tell you what to do, so you can live your life in your own way

Cons

- Although most of the people enjoy being alone, this is not true most of the time
- Silence can be sometimes irritating for some people

- You may need to have someone to talk to but you're alone and sometimes the silence is deafening
- Sometimes you will feel completely alone, feel loneliness, lack of company, even though the truth is that most of the times you will really be alone
- Loneliness and lack of company, along with a daily routine make life boring
- By nature, humans are social beings
- There is none to console you when you are down or to help you in a case of emergency, if, for example, you slip and fall, or if you want to lift something heavy, hang stuff, or build a bed, you have to invite people to help you
- You have to maintain cleanness of the house on your own. It is always your turn to clean the bathroom, there is none there to clean out the fridge for you
- When living alone, you will be responsible for all the bills, as there is none to split expenses with
- It is more expensive because you have to pay all the rent and bills yourself
- It is quite hard to find a nice and affordable flat for one person in the city centre
- You might not be able to live in the area you would like to
- Living alone is better for older people who have more money and like privacy but not for young people who need to share the costs
- Staying alone sometimes makes you feel insecure (a feeling of lack of safety)
- People who experience problems and live alone may not have an outlet to talk about them

15.7. Living with your Family or Relative Members

Pros

- Living at your parents' home provides you the luxury of having the time to sit and think extensively about what you want to do with your life, study, your prospective career decisions, allowing you to be more flexible about the decisions you can make
- You save yourself a lot of time by not having to think about household chores as it would be if you lived alone
- Saving money is the most common reason people move in with their family
- Financial issues during hard times are in general fewer for those living in multi-generational households than for people living alone
- You can save a lot of money on rent, utility bills, renovations, shared grocery bills, and a lot more
- You may contribute to the household expenses, but in any case you would spend more if you were on your own
- You have the freedom to take more risks and make better decisions. For example, if you are on your own, the pressure to pay the bills might force you to accept the first job offer you get, and not wait for a better offer

- You can focus more on your studies, as you will not be burdened by concerns such as cooking and cleaning leaves you plenty of room for long, uninterrupted study sessions
- Living with relatives can increase your happiness, as it develops wonderful family bonds
- There is always someone around that can help you in any kind of big or small problem, or with your kids
- You will not have to do all the housework (laundry) as there are a lot more hands to the work
- Living with your parents means you can enjoy warm, home-cooked meals even when you do not have time to cook

- Your privacy will be compromised, as well as you will provided with abundance of unsolicited advice on how to live your life
- Living with your parents means that you are likely to receive all kinds of advice, even if you do not ask for it
- Even though a large number of students do stay home, there is a prevailing belief that they can grown-up only if they live alone, or else they will be behind in the race to be independent and self-reliant. Staying at home means that you might have to deal with the social stigma of living with your parents
- Moving in with relatives and sharing living space with parents or siblings can lead to more family conflicts and confrontations
- You cannot call friends over or host house parties at any time you want
- Your parents will always treat you as their child

15.8. Reality TV Shows

- Some shows are similar to traditional television variety or talent shows providing a showcase for talented young models and artists
- For some participants, these shows become a steppingstone to a successful career
- Reality TV shows may address numerous social issues and introduce people to the problems plaguing the society
- Some reality programs show real people struggling with drug and alcohol addictions, displaying the cold and cruel face of addiction without making it glamorous

- Many forms of reality TV programs have little to do with reality, they are not that real at all
- Some reality programs give the impression that these shows are unscripted and natural, but the truth is that most reality shows are tightly scripted and controlled and stories and situations are developed in advance
- Most reality TV shows spotlight bad behavior, meanness, greed, deception and other negative personality traits
- Oftentimes, the winners of these shows are those who have the least amount of moral scruples
- Reality TV shows influence young people negatively, not providing any positive influences at all
- They provide a negative role-model as often violent upheavals among members of the groups are shown, vile language usage is a common place, and the participant make money quickly and easily
- Reality TV shows are vulgar and shoddy and create pseudo-celebrities
- Oftentimes, they exploit the vulnerable only in order to gain more number of viewers
- Many reality shows just try to create dramas

15.9. Reality TV Shows and Children

Effects

- Many children sacrifice endless hours for rehearsals to train in their artistic pursuit
- If young children fail to get selected, or been proclaimed talented, end up in great emotional trauma
- Telling young contestants that they are devoid of talent is heartbreaking
- Children won talent contests and become celebrity miss out on carefree childhood experiences, are forced to lead an adult lifestyle, and constantly face the fear of public rejection
- When the glory of fame fades out, children became frustrated, bewildered, and bitterly disappointed
- Children academic performance is adversely influenced

Reasons

- Talent competitions put contestants under pressure and stress which children are not properly equipped to deal with

- As most children are too young to know whether they really want to participate in such shows or not they entrust this responsibility to their parents or guardians and they act according to their own desires
- Children are not able to handle the consequences of these shows, even if they win and achieve sudden fame, let alone when they lose
- Fame, and in particular children fame, is short-living
- Winning in such talent contests may be far more damaging than being defeated, as this could easily result in loss of kids' innocence

15.10. Poverty

Causes

- Poverty is an exceptionally complicated social phenomenon, and trying to discover its causes is equally complicated
- Lack of education, high divorce rate, a culture of poverty, overpopulation, epidemic diseases such as AIDS and malaria, environmental problems such as lack of rainfall, are some of the main causes of poverty. Additionally,
- Multifold increase in population without equal increase in job creation
- Unemployment and not generating sufficient employment
- Natural disasters and extreme weather may be a cause of poverty in many countries
- Drought, rainfall and flooding are some of the biggest causes of poverty
- The inability of poor households to invest in property and education, the limited access to credit, produce more poverty via inherited poverty
- Physical or mental disability, being part of a lone-parent family, and having less than a high school education can result in poverty even in rich countries
- War evict people from their homes and deprive them of food and shelter, and services such as hospitals, schools, gas, water and electricity
- War and violence, political violence and organized crime have affected many countries in the world, resulting in higher poverty level than in non-violent countries
- Overpopulation and underdevelopment do not allow enough wealth per capita to be created so that poor people to be able to escape from poverty
- Not using upgraded technology but following conventional agriculture farming leads to low produce and low income
- In addition, division and sub-division of agriculture land leads to small farms with low production
- When natural disasters do not gain media attention raising money the situation becomes really difficult.
- The poor's living conditions are made worse when governments spend money in the capital, an usually rich enough region, instead of the poorest areas which need it most

- Poverty and violence also feed themselves
- A country's low economy due poor labor market leads the poor to be exploited with very low wages
- Increasing food prices due to changes in commodity prices policies increase the poverty rate
- Slow economic growth contributes to the persistence of poverty and non-poor people become poor
- Unemployment, causes families to live in unsanitary conditions because a lack of financial means to improve living conditions deteriorating their poverty

- **Hunger, illness and thirst are both causes and effects of poverty**
- If the parents are unemployed, this can also affect how their children are brought up and what kind of education they receive
- Extreme poverty may affect lifespan
- Children who grow up in poverty suffer more persistent, frequent, and severe health problems than do children who grow up under better financial circumstances
- Many infants born into poverty have a low birth weight, associated with many preventable mental and physical disabilities
- Poor infants are not only more likely to be irritable and sickly, but they are also more likely to die before their first birthday
- Children raised in poverty tend to miss school more often because of illness
- The levels of stress in poor families is higher
- Poor families experience much more stress than middle-class families
- Job loss and subsequent poverty are associated with violence in families, including child and elder abuse
- Besides financial uncertainty, poor families are more likely to be exposed to illnesses, depression, eviction, job loss, and criminal victimization
- Parents having hard economic difficulties may become excessively punitive and erratic, issuing demands backed by insults, threats, and corporal punishment
- Extreme poverty carries with it a particularly strong set of risks for families, especially children
- Poor children are less likely to receive proper nutrition and immunization, and, therefore, they experience more health problems

- Poverty can be reduced with the creation of social security programs or offering a universal pension
- World leaders should conduct peaceful negotiation instead of dealing problems with war

- Creation of organizations/programs to absorb labor and provide income for poor families can ameliorate the problem
- Massive aid from the rest of the world should be provided to poor countries
- Providing employment to the poor so that they have a regular income on a monthly basis
- All efforts should be made to increase the employment opportunities in the poor countries, either by inviting more foreign investments or by encouraging self-employment schemes
- The population growth at the current rate should be checked by implementing policies and awareness that promote birth control
- Free high school education and an increased number of functioning health centers should be provided by the governments to the poor

15.11. Homelessness

Causes

- Many homeless individual failed in their lives to cope with difficulties and this makes them alienate themselves from the rest of the world
- Foreclosure increase the number of people who experience homelessness
- Homelessness and poverty are inextricably linked
- Poor people are frequently unable to pay for housing, as well as food, childcare, health care, and education
- Eroding work opportunities, including stagnant or falling incomes and less secure jobs, lead to homelessness
- Domestic violence in poor families, often battered women, forces people to choose between abusive relationships and homelessness
- Mental illnesses is a significant contributor to homelessness
- Serious mental illnesses disrupt people's ability to carry out essential aspects of daily life, such as self-care and household management, and may prevent people from forming and maintaining stable relationships

Effects

- The effects of homelessness on homeless people range from health issues to personal entrapment
- Homeless people often encounter a lot of health issues in their lives
- Homeless people health gets worse from time to time because they lack attention from other people such as doctors, wives, husbands, and family members
- Because of lack of necessities many homeless people may suffer from multiple diseases such as:
  - Cold Injury
  - Cardio-Respiratory diseases

- o Tuberculosis
- o Skin diseases
- o Nutritional deficiencies
- o Sleep deprivation
- o Mental illness
- o Physical and sexual assault
- o Drug dependency
- o Mortality
- o HIV/AIDS
- Homeless people also suffer psychologically
- They may experience a loss of self esteem, become institutionalized, end up in substance misuse, or lose their ability and will to care for themselves
- Homeless people may develop behavioral problems, display increased danger of abuse and violence, or increased chance of entering the criminal justice system
- For many people being homeless mean spent sleeping rough, living in hostels and/or moving between different types of accommodation
- Being homeless may mean not having a normal family life or social contacts and a lack of belonging
- Long-term homelessness can impact on a person's self-esteem, and deprive them of the opportunity to do well in education or employment

Solutions to chronic homelessness

- Making drug and alcohol abuse services and treatments readily available to homeless individuals suffering from substance addiction gives them a greater chance to recover and begin the path back to a normal, stable life
- To recover homeless individuals with mental disorders or physical disabilities, they need professional and affordable medical treatment
- The most effective means of preventing chronic homelessness is to make available permanent supportive housing that provides a safe and healthy environment for homeless individuals
- Governments should implement measures and develop programs that make homeless people to feel secure and a productive member of the community

15.12. Juvenile Delinquency

Reasons/Causes

- Most of the adolescents who show delinquent behavior in any form belong to families that could not give their children firm foundation
- Broken families, single parent families, separated families, frequent parents fight, lack of trust and confidence among the parents, criminal parents or psychological problems in parents can be the most important reason behind juvenile delinquency

- Siblings' rivalry or unequal treatment between children is another possible reason
- Economic problems in family often cause juvenile delinquency
- Youth from poor economical status families easily get involved in criminal activities
- Poor young people want to improve their status and for this reason they resort to negative paths and criminal activities
- Psychological problems, like mental illnesses, depression, frustration, aggression or hyper behavior, in family, in parents or siblings, can also lead to juvenile delinquency
- Parents or elder siblings involved in social problems like gender discrimination, age discrimination, racial discrimination, child labor or violation of animal rights may cause stress and due to these stress teens get involved in violence
- Wrong parenting may be one of the biggest reasons why teens commit crime. For example, parents may be very harsh and punish their children for **small/trivial** issues
- Racial differences can cause juvenile delinquency, as adolescents become aggressive and want to take revenge for the unequal treatment that the society or the other people shows to them
- Drug use is a very common cause of juvenile delinquency
- Juveniles who use drugs usually get involved in criminal activities as most of their friends belong to criminal class
- Peer group influence or rejection can cause delinquent behavior in the adolescent, as it is a very strong force
- Adolescents can show delinquent behavior when they cannot get similar resources as their friends have
- Being part of a clique may force teens adopt abusive behavior and get involved in negative acts, even in committing crimes

Solution

- Parents and elder siblings should provide the younger member of the family with positive values, norms and standards so that they will be able to adopt the right behavior to the society
- The family should have a positive attitude towards life and society values
- Government should support families that have poor economic status so that they can improve their financial condition and prevent their children from resorting to criminal behavior
- Parents should teach their children the importance of respecting the law by letting them know the consequences of breaking it
- In case of disability, parents and teachers should discuss with the teens about their situation and try to solve any problem they face
- Parents should ensure that their children are hanging out with friends who belong to their class and to respectable families, as this can prevent adolescent jealousy which in turn it may lead to delinquent behavior

- To avoid peer group influence on teens, parents should know the friends of their children and create a healthy and friendly relationship with their kids so that they can feel free to share all their thoughts with their parents

15.13. Obsession with Appearance: Plastic Surgery

Reasons/Causes

- As appearance and self-image are very important for many people, driven by an inferiority complex some people suffer from obsession with physical appearance and lack in self-esteem and try to enhance it with appearance improvements
- Possible good results boost self-confidence
- Peer pressure plays a central role
- Young people do not want to stand out from the crowd, but to comply with the ideal image of perfection. Therefore, they struggle to meet "acceptable" standards of appearance by improving appearance imperfections
- Media exert a strong influence on what real beauty is, and as young people are bombarded with images of anorexic young bodies, many women result in never being satisfied with any "flaws" they may have
- On the other hand, re-constructive surgery for car accident victims or people who are born with abnormalities is justifiable

Effects

- Many operations are performed only for the sake of vanity or self-image
- Plastic surgery often has numerous unwanted repercussions, as it rarely is a simple procedure
- Many times the end results are very different from what was initially desired, and sometimes they are dangerous too
- There are plenty of cases where patients suffer permanent disfigurement after having undergone such a operation
- Some people, especially (young) women, enter an endless vicious cycle of remedial surgery, as they become addicted to the process of flaws correcting and "perfecting" themselves
- Some people after having undergone an plastic surgery fall into deeper depression as they discover that nothing in their lives has actually changed despite the fact they have eliminated the reason of their unhappiness: have corrected the feature of their body they thought was responsible for it (unhappiness)

15.14. Teenage smokers

Reasons/Causes

- Adolescence is a time of rebellion
- Teenagers are generally aware that their parents disapprove of smoking and this makes many of them want to do it more
- Young people often give in to negative peer pressure
- Since their friends smoke they do not like to feel different
- They often think it makes them look cool, especially when they see famous people such as pop stars on TV smoking

Effects

- Recent anti-smoking campaigns have done very little to combat the issue
- The government should use adverts with clean-living sports personalities and celebrities to demonstrate the negative effects of smoking and show teenagers that not to smoke is cooler
- Personalities with admirable qualities should take part in anti-smoking campaigns, to persuade the young quit smoking

15.15. Vandalism

Reasons

- Many teenagers become vandals because they have no other outlet for their anger or frustration
- They try to do something daring or dangerous to show their friends they are cool
- Sometimes when teenagers are in a group, they do things they probably would not do when alone

Solutions

- Patrol the public parks and downtown areas more, especially at night
- Seeing more police officers around will surely discourage vandals from destroying public property
- Form citizens' groups that would keep their eyes open and call the police as soon as they see vandals
- Organize a competition for graffiti artists. In this way, the paintings would be of better quality and not on every wall in town, eliminating this type of vandalism

Effects

- Refugees often suffer badly from racism and prejudices in the host country
- It is sometimes better for the refugees to receive aid in their native land than begging on the streets in a country where they cannot even speak the language
- Many so-called economic migrants end up returning to the country of their birth

Actions to tackle the problem

- Industrialized countries should help by allowing higher levels of immigration and providing real integration of refugees
- Acceptance of more immigrants is essential, particularly when immigration is caused by natural disasters or civil war
- In general, immigration has caused more problems than it has solved
- Developed nations should help poor countries overcome their economic problems as we now live in a globalized world and it is no longer possible to ignore what happens on the other side of it

16. Topic Questions

1. Media follow famous people, such as footballers, film stars and politicians, any aspect of their life. **Do these people deserve to have a private life without journalists constantly following them? Discuss your point of view and support it with examples.**

2. Some people think that child stars need protection from the media. Others say they don't. **What do you think? Explain your opinion, giving specific reasons to support your view.**

3. Some people think that it is beneficial for teenagers to have a part-time job instead of extra-curricular activities. **Could a job like this help students or it would create extra problems for them during the school year? Support your views with examples.**

4. Some people believe that it is important for young people to learn to earn money early in their life rather than being given pocket money. **Do you agree, or not with statement? Support your viewpoint.**

5. While it may cause serious problems in the family when both parents work, in the long term, it can make their life easier. **Discuss the advantages and disadvantages of both parents working and the effects this has on the family.**

6. In the last decades the number of students who decide to study abroad has been increased. **What are the advantages and disadvantages of the decision to study abroad?**

7. Many parents are concerned about what their children watch on television but do not know what to do about it. **How can parents be sure that their children are watching acceptable programs? Write an essay making suggestions by giving examples.**

8. Watching Television has advantages, is it an entertainment medium, but also disadvantages, if it is overused. **Describe how television affects the people who choose to watch it. Do you think the effects are positive or negative?**

9.   Some people believe that many children spend too much time on the Internet and playing computer games. **What are the advantages and disadvantages of this action?**

10. It is often said that young people today do not care about anything else except for their own interests such as fashion and music. **Do you agree with this statement or not? What is your own opinion on this matter? Give examples.**

11. Fashion industry has a bad effect on people's lives. **Do you agree, or not with statement? Support your viewpoint.**

12. **Why it is a good to include** physical exercise **in our daily schedule?**

13. **What can parents do to help their children** eat **better? Suggest ways parents can follow to improve their children' habits and help them lead a healthier lifestyle. Be specific.**

14. **Do you think** parents **should be very** protective **of their children and make all the decisions, or they should give their children responsibility from a young age? Which approach do you believe is correct?**

15. **Why some times** young people **run away from home and end up on the streets? Give examples of some of the** problems **young people could face while trying to survive on the streets and suggest some ways in which they could be helped.**

16. Many kids experience peer pressure. **What are the most common reasons? Do you think that teens need adult support in order to deal with peer pressure successfully? What must be done in order to avoid peer pressure? Give examples to support your opinion.**

17. There are many teens that stay in difficult relationships, with peer pressure be a common experience nowadays. Some believe that self-esteem plays a large role in this. **What are some other ways can help teens cope with difficult friendships? Discuss your point of view and support it with examples.**

18. Bullying is on the rise in schools of many countries of the world. **How do bullying affects the victims? Should bullies be expelled from school? Give your views on this issue and explain it.**

19. Friends are an important part of every people's life. **What do you think are the most important reasons, and what qualities young people should look for in their friends? Give examples.**

20. At some of their life most teenagers have problems with their parents. **What are the reasons? What can be done by both young people and their parents to make their cohabitation and thus their life easier?**

21. It is generally acknowledged people's lifestyle in cities is hectic and unhealthy causing them a number of psychological and physical ailments. **What can cities' authorities do in order to help their citizens feel more relaxed and entertained? Support your views with examples.**

22. **What can people do to help** protect the environment, **and why should they do so?**

23. Although there are recycling bins almost in any place, very few people have really supported this action. **Why are not people enthusiastic about recycling? How can we encourage more people to become actively involved with the protection of the environment?**

24. A good way to protect our environment and to save public money is to recycle our trash. However, few people are involved consciously. **What can be done to persuade people to recycle their trash responsibly? Support your ideas with examples.**

25. Many people choose to get to their workplace or school by driving their own car, whereas others are using public transport systems. **What factors affect their decision? Give details to explain your choice.**

26. **Should there be special regulations about where** motorbikes **can and cannot be driven? Or, should motorbikes simply obey the same rules as cars do? Explain, giving specific reasons to support your opinion.**

27. Drink-driving is a very irresponsible act and a serious problem which can have severe consequences, both for the drivers and for the passengers. **What can be done to stop people using their cars after they have been drinking alcohol? Support your ideas with examples.**

28. Pollution is a phenomenon that has been proven particularly hazardous for our health. **What can be done to reduce this problem and make citizens' lives more enjoyable? Support your ideas with examples.**

29. Environment pollution and damage is a common problem in many countries in the world. **Do you think these problems can be solved?**

30. Many of our seas and rivers are polluted. **What are some of the causes of the problem and what could be done to improve this situation?**

31. Some people claim that animals exist on this planet only for human's use. Therefore, it is not wrong to kill them either for food or for clothing. Whereas others say that it is not right to kill animals for any reason. **Discuss these two viewpoints and give your own opinion.**

32. Some people believe that spending public tax money to improve professional sports teams' facilities, e.g. stadiums, is justified, whereas others think that only team owners should pay for their stadium improvements. **What do you think? Explain your opinion, giving specific reasons to support your view.**

33. **Should governments or societies spend too much time and money on sports, or should they use these resources on arts and science? Explain your viewpoint by giving specific reasons to support it.**

34. **Is it good for the countries to spend a lot of money on their heritage? Give reasons to support your point of view.**

35. Too much money is spent on education and not enough on sports facilities. **Do you agree or disagree with this statement. Give examples to support your views. Be specific.**

36. **How do you think could science be made more appealing to young people, and why should it be appealing? Give reasons to support your point of view.**

37. Can women do any job men can do? **Are there jobs women cannot or should not do? Give your opinion supporting your view point with examples.**

38. The problem of young people becoming addicted to drugs is more serious now than ever. In order to combat this problem, some people propose drugs to be made legal so that to lose their attraction. **Do you agree with this viewpoint? Explain your views on this subject with examples.**

39. Recently, the trafficking of illegal drugs, both to adolescents and to adults, has become a particularly serious problem in many big cities of the world. **What can be done to reduce this problem and make our cities a safer place to live for all citizens? Support your ideas with examples.**

40. Most of us have had the experience of being near someone who was using a cell phone impolitely in public space. **Do you think cell phone use in public is a serious problem or just an occasional annoyance? Give examples to support your opinion.**

41. **What are the advantages and disadvantages of shopping at very large supermarkets in relation to shopping in small, local stores? Give specific examples to support your answer.**

42. **Should popular** tourist destination **be protected from very large numbers of visitors? Or should they be used to the most in order for the local community to be able to benefit as much as possible? Explain your views and support them by giving specific reasons and examples.**

43. Cheap mass tourism has both its advantages and disadvantages. **Describe how this form of tourism can affect the poorer countries of the world. Do you think the effects are positive or negative?**

44. **What are the advantages and disadvantages of** buying products coming from other countries? **Should we stop doing it and start buying only locally produced goods and services so, or not?**

45. Should shops be open 24 hours a day, seven days a week? **Give your point of view providing reasons to support it.**

46. Whereas prison remains the most common form of punishment for most criminals, some people believe that there should be used other options and methods. **How else could criminals be punished and what are other possible ways of persuading people not to commit crimes again in the future? Support your ideas with examples.**

47. Cigarettes and alcohol are dangerous products, and, therefore, there should be a complete ban on their advertising. **Do you agree with this view or not? Where are cigarettes and alcohol currently advertised? Who is influenced by these adverts? Would a "complete" ban be effective? Would it discourage people from smoking or drinking?**

48. Is it better to live alone or with someone else? **What are the advantages and disadvantages of each option?**

Vocabulary Notes

Word/Phrase   **Meaning**

Vocabulary Notes

Word/Phrase	Meaning

Vocabulary Notes

Word/Phrase   **Meaning**

Vocabulary Notes

Word/Phrase   **Meaning**

Vocabulary Notes

Word/Phrase   **Meaning**

Vocabulary Notes

Word/Phrase	Meaning

Vocabulary Notes

Word/Phrase   **Meaning**

Vocabulary Notes

Word/Phrase   **Meaning**

Vocabulary Notes

<table>
<tr><th>Word/Phrase</th><th>Meaning</th></tr>
</table>

Vocabulary Notes

Word/Phrase	Meaning

Vocabulary Notes

Word/Phrase	Meaning

Vocabulary Notes

Word/Phrase	Meaning

Vocabulary Notes

Word/Phrase   **Meaning**

Vocabulary Notes

Word/Phrase   **Meaning**

Vocabulary Notes

Word/Phrase	**Meaning**

Vocabulary Notes

Word/Phrase   **Meaning**

Vocabulary Notes

Word/Phrase	Meaning

Vocabulary Notes

Word/Phrase   **Meaning**

About the Author

Stavros Krathanasis has a strong background in science and excellent writing skills, being particularly proficient in scientific writing. His experience has been gained through secondary school and postgraduate teaching, postdoctoral academic research, working in the academic publishing industry, as well as through long-time career in the Public Administration. He has more than 15 years of experience as independent writer, being a published author in the fields of science, and he has also served as a reviewer for paper to be published in academic conferences.

Poor documentation, clarifications and explanations is a common problem in many written works. As an experienced writer, as well as an academic teacher, he knows that it takes a great attention to detail in order to tackle even the most common errors and mistakes regularly made by writers. He has successfully assisted and supervised postgraduate students to achieve positive outcomes from their written work, as well as help them polish their theses and papers so that they are error-free and beautifully structured.

The author's qualifications include a Bachelor of Science (Physics), a Master of Science in Environmental Physics, a Ph.D. in Physics, as well as a Certificate of Proficiency in English from the University of Michigan. He is fluent in English and German, has an excellent command of grammar. Because he has written many books in English and have faced the difficult task to understand the work of writers whose first language is not English, he can cope successfully with the difficulties faced by writer who use English as a Second Language (ESL).

www.ingramcontent.com/pod-product-compliance
Lightning Source LLC
LaVergne TN
LVHW080416200726

843506LV00004B/308